D1882887

KURUKSHETRA
The Battle Royale

KURUKSHETRA

Ramdhari Singh 'Dinkar'

The Battle Royale

An adaptation in rhymed English verse
by

Dr. Shachi Kant **Dr. Raman P. Singh**

Vani

A Creative Imprint of Vani Prakashan

New Delhi

www.vaniprakashan.in

VANI PRAKASHAN

4695, 21-A, Daryaganj, New Delhi 110 002

Branch

Ashok Rajpath, Patna 800 004

Phone : +91 11 23273167 Fax : +91 11 23275710

www.vaniprakashan.in
vaniprakashan@gmail.com

KURUKSHETRA
(in Hindi)
by
Ramdhari Singh 'Dinkar'

Adapted in English as
THE BATTLE ROYALE
by
Dr. Shachi Kant, Dr. Raman P. Singh

ISBN : 978-93-5072-414-9
Poetry

© 2013 Arvind Kumar Singh
Translation © Dr. Shachi Kant, Dr. Raman P. Singh

First Edition

Price : ₹ 250

Kurukshetra : The Battle Royale is published by Vani Prakashan and copyrighted in 2013 to Arvind Kumar Singh & Translation © Dr. Shachi Kant, Dr. Raman P. Singh. All rights reserved. No part of this book may be reproduced, in any form by any machanical or electronic means (including photocopying, recording or information storage or reprinted) without permission in writing from publisher. Users are not allowed to mount this file on any network servers including e-mail.

Printed at Om Offset Platemaking, Delhi 110 093

Vani Prakashan's signature motif is created by Artist Maqbool Fida Husain

Peace can't reign supreme unless the share
Of human happiness be fair and square,
None should have too much 'n' more,
None else too little for his own score.

"Which is better, strength or reason?
Is the sword best, or is it persuasion?
Which is better, the blood-besmirched feat,
Or the dire, dismal, death-bringing defeat?

Preface

Kurukshetra has not been written in the manner of *Mahabharata* composed by sage Veda Vyas, nor re-telling the great epic was my motive. Whatever it was that I intended to convey could as well have been expressed without referring to the discourse between Yudhishthira and Bhisma. In that case, however, the poem would have lost its epical dimensions; it would have instead become a collection of so many miniature songs. Nevertheless, the fact remains that I had no definite plan to shape it into an epical mould. In fact, it so happened that the renunciation of great Emperor Ashok fascinated me; and while writing the poem *Kalinga Vijay* (*Victory of Kalinga*) a firm conviction grew upon me: the conviction that the problem of war is at the root of all ills plaguing humanity. From this perspective, while reflecting over the Dwapar age, I found Yudhishthira weighing 'victory' (a petty word) against the dead bodies lying scattered all across the battlefield of Kurukshetra. Yet, there is another aspect of the question that looms large in the morality-hued statements of Bhisma. The battle of soul is won by the soul, and that of the body by the body. This story pertains to the end of the war. The import of what Lord Krishna had spoken to Arjuna before the onset of the battle was not to resort to austerity and penance in the face of injustice.

War is surely a condemnable and cruel act, but upon whom lies its onus? Upon him who weaves a net of inequities and invites retaliation thence? Or, upon him who is determined to tear asunder that dragnet to bits? Apparently, Duryodhana manipulated to create a sham regime of peace — albeit by banishing the Pandavas from the kingdom. Should not have Prince Yudhishthira tried to oppose such imposed peace?

These were some of the issues and gradual reflection over these culminated into the fruition of this poem. By taking the prop of Bhisma and Yudhishthira I have presented the pros and cons of this mind-boggling question in the manner I could comprehend it. Hence, I do not claim that Bhisma and Yudhishthira, as portrayed in *Kurukshetra*, are the replicas of Bhisma and Yudhishthira of *Mahabharata*. Nevertheless, I have exercised utmost caution all through the poem that these characters do not utter anything that is not in conformity with the spirit of the Dwapar age. However, I have taken the liberty to articulate in a novel and elaborate manner wherever Bhisma narrates something that resonates with the pulse of our age. At places, I have indulged in assumption for the replies Bhisma Pitamaha would have given to questions similar to those confronting him in the hoary past. Indeed the dictum "what does not exist in India does not exist beyond India" is a truism. Ever since I read about Bhisma's notions of society without kingship and the scorched earth policy, I have become entrenched in these beliefs all the more.

I do take upon myself the blame for wherever my imagination has soared but deviated to a plane that does not dovetail with the spirit of the Dwapar age. The readers can easily discern such references which are conspicuous due to their brevity. The whole of Canto VI belongs to this category which can live on its own as a separate work even if severed from this poem.

Before I conclude I would like to submit that the unity of epical dimensions in *Kurukshetra* stems from the thoughts described therein. To be candid, I have been pondering over all this while writing this book. The poem merges into Bhisma, as it were, once it has arrived at him. The fact remains, however, that *Kurukshetra* is neither a treatise on philosophy nor a product of a mature and wise mind. In its essence, it is the venting out of a commoner's anguished heart expressing itself at the level of the mind. So be it.

Ramdhari Singh 'Dinkar'

Translators' Note

Kurukshetra is regarded in the annals of Hindi poetry as a *piece de resistance*, a great masterpiece of ideas and thoughts; and its architect, Ramdhari Singh 'Dinkar', is recognized as one of the greatest Hindi poets of his time. It is Dinkar's *magnum opus*, a poem that rises head and shoulders above his early poems, revealing the triumph of his mature art, an art which is remarkable as much for its orchestral swelling and flourishing as for its depth and discipline. Dinkar himself considered *Kurukshetra* to be his greatest work, even though he bagged the highest literary award in India (*Bharatiya Jnanpith*) for *Urvashi* (*The Celestial Damsel*). The poem is indeed an epic-in-miniature; it is full of thoughts that breathe, and words that burn. The poet's feelings are always firmly grounded to the demands and ideas of the heroic form. In other words, there is an unexceptionable substratum of thought beneath every flight of eloquence. The first thing that strikes the reader of *Kurukshetra* is its breathtaking clarity, a clarity which is produced by a sense of order, not by an undirected originality. There is nothing of the misty here, nothing of the incoherent. It is this 'noble conception', this grandness of theme, coupled with the native genius of the poet, which so delighted Dinkar's readers and won their affection.

Kurukshetra is a coming forward to the realm of the impersonal and the universal; it is a break-away from the haphazard and the idiosyncratic as well as from the shapeless and the individualistic. The philosophy of life enunciated here is immensely down-to-earth and pragmatic. It pivots on the representation of the eternal conflict between worldliness and renunciation, violence and non-violence, war and peace, and similar pairs of opposites. The most interesting thing about the poem is that it is an endeavour to reconcile opposites in the realm of thought, a striking of balance, a dance of the contrapuntal, as it were. Dinkar's mastery lies in describing an immediately contemporary and time-bound experience in words that are timeless and emotions that are eternal. He makes an affirmation of hope and belief by averring that social and economic equality as well as a general diffusion of prosperity can alone ensure world peace. He evokes the strong-among-the-ordinary to become morally strong to persuade the politician and the scientist to submit to the laws of society and humanity; otherwise, science will continue to intensify rather than to mitigate the evils of tyranny and war. Like Shelley, the poet urges us

To suffer woes which Hope thinks infinite:
To forgive wrongs darker than death or night:
To defy Power, which seems omnipotent;
To love, and bear; to hope till Hope creates
From its own wreck the thing it contemplates;
Neither to change, nor falter, nor repent.

As Tulsidas rejuvenated the Muse of Valmiki in his *Ramcharitmanas*, so has Dinkar revitalized the Inspirer of Veda Vyas in *Kurukshetra*. The poet here indulges in thoughts with ease, traces the features of the hoary Mahabharata war and its aftermath, makes it rich with sublime ideas, infuses the rare music of the Muse in the story, and thus consecrates the poem with the breath of life to make it eternal in its appeal. Though *Kurukshetra* is not an epic by accepted standards, it has several of its attributes - the principal one being the portrayal of the age-old conflict between the individualistic and the personal preoccupation on the one hand as well as the social and the impersonal urge on the other. In this and other aspects, the poem reminds us of such splendid pieces of English poetry as Milton's *Samson Agonistes* and Shelley's *Prometheus Unbound.* In the Aristotelian sense, *Kurukshetra* has a noble conception, a grand theme (the aftermath of a terrible war), sublime characters, and stately imagery; while the poet's Muse remains queenly as Cleopatra, even while she takes the asp of cold philosophy to her heart.

Kurukshetra is thus an epic-in-miniature on war and peace. It is a rendition of the eternal, acute and intense problem plaguing the human civilization since the days of yore. The human mind has ever been in search of an effective pill for the ills of war, an anodyne that would bring in a permanent reign of peace. The craving for a society in which injustice and inequity are banned has ever been the ideal goal of the philosopher and of the poet, as it has ever been the dream of the humankind in general. A serious discussion on various causative factors of war, fixation of the responsibility of initiating war, the concomitants of peace etc form the heart of the matter in *Kurukshetra*. The poem's speciality consists in a series of dialogues loaded with forceful thoughts encased in powerful words with myriad hues that further add to the effect of thoughts.

As a meditative epic on war and peace, *Kurukshetra* symbolizes the final break of the new poet from the ennui and the individualistic preoccupation of the *chhayavadi* (romantic) poets. It marks the turning-point of Hindi poetry from the introvertistic attitude of its predecessors and may be regarded as a milestone in Hindi literature. It is not as if this poem provides an intellectually satisfying answer, from the progressive standpoint, to the cardinal problem facing its author. A poem which seeks to do that ceases to be a poem, as is apparent from the numerous flat pieces of Sumitra Nandan Pant in *Gramya* (The Village Deity) and *Yugavani* (The Voice of the Age). *Kurukshetra* does something different; it invokes the spirit of doubt, and through epical imagery, lofty characterization, and emotional fervence stimulates in the reader the mood of receptivity for the eternal message of hope and faith. The poet's greatest success lies in the creation of moods rather than a succession of moods.

Kurukshetra reveals the heroic India to the world, an India hitherto in oblivion. The contents of the poem have remained restricted to the Hindi-knowing readers till date. In rendering the mini-epic in rhymed English verse, the authors are acting as facilitators, or rather as bridge-builders. After going through it, the reader is bound to agree with Max Mueller's opinion:

> *If I were asked under what sky the human mind has most fully developed some of its choicest gifts, has most deeply pondered*

on the greatest problems of life, and has found solutions, I should point to India.

Romain Rolland, too, echoed the same sentiments when he observed: *If there is one place on the face of earth where all the dreams of living men have found a home from the very earliest days when man began the dream of existence, it is India.*

Other great Indologists and Indophiles, like Mark Twain, have considered India to be *the cradle of human race, the birth place of human speech, the mother of history, the grandmother of legend and the great-grandmother of tradition.* Dinkar's *Kurukshetra* in very many ways epitomizes the spirit of these statements.

The adaptation of Kurukshetra in English verse by the authors was inspired by our mentor, the late lamented Professor Ram Khelawan Roy (Ex. Head, Department of Hindi, Patna University). Famously known in the academia as 'Gurudeva' (Revered Teacher), Professor Roy was a erudite scholar of Sanskrit, Hindi, Indic philosophy, spirituality and culture. It is chiefly to him that we are indebted for the subject itself as well as for encouragement and sagacious suggestions. It has taken a while to accomplish the fruition of this work, as all such things do, but the delay has been a blessing in disguise, as in the intervening years the work has become more fine-tuned and yet better-honed, making it — we hope — enormously readable. Certainly, we owe it to our mentor for inspiring us to writhe in the labour of love and produce this piece of work which transçends the frontiers of translation. The endeavour to mould *Kurukshetra* into English verse also stems from the need to apprise the English-knowing literati about the ideas treasured in this modern epic of Dinkar who is held in the highest esteem by Hindi readers for the depth of his vision, imagination and thought. The rendering of the modern Hindi epic in English verse has been achieved without any dilution of thought or meaning inherent in the original Hindi poem in any manner. We do not hesitate to state that moulding *Kurukshetra* into rhymed English verse has been an enormous task, a mind-churning and nerve-straining endeavour, as the diction of the great twentieth century Hindi poet is unique and exemplary. We have tried to keep pace with the force of poet's thoughts, embedded in a mesmerically flowing language, which gains in momentum as the epical story progresses. The themes and thoughts (war and peace) that vibrate all through this great work are perpetual in their appeal which make the poet and his poetry contemporaneous in this age of rampant violence, terrorism and confusion over deteriorating human values.

Through this trans-creation India salutes Dinkar and gives signal honour to the nobility of thoughts as contained in *Kurukshetra*. We have persevered to recreate the effect of *Kurukshetra's* thoughts, in a language with a variety of rhymes and rhythms that make a direct appeal to the hearts and minds of English readers, as Dinkar was a poet passionately in love with language, a master of the art and craft of expression. Keeping pace with the craftsmanship of such a masterly poet has been a real challenge to the authors. It is up to the discerning literati, as well as to the lay readers, to decide whether justice has been done to the original work in this trans-creation. In the meanwhile, we offer this work, a labour of love, as a homage to Dinkar, one of the greatest Hindi poets of modern times.

II

Kurukshetra is a district in the state of Haryana in India presently experiencing a tourist boom. In itself, the term Kurukshetra is a geographical expression for the lands lying between the two rivers namely Saraswati and Drishadvati, and is referred to in the ancient *Vaman Purana* as the land where King Kuru of the Bharat Dynasty settled down for earning spiritual merit. Lord Vishnu, the Hindu god, impressed by Kuru's austerities, bestowed him with a couple of boons – one, that this land Kurukshetra (the land of Kuru) forever will be known as a holy land after his name; and, other, that anyone dying on this land will go directly to heaven. Later, the great war of Mahabharata was fought on this land between Pandavas and Kauravas, the descendents of King Kuru, for supremacy to the throne of Hastinapur (modern Delhi). When the Mahabharata war was declared and the two armies faced each other, Lord Krishna (an incarnation of Vishnu) preached *Bhagavad Gita* to Arjuna, one of the five Pandava brothers and the greatest archer of his age, and instructed him not to yield to the terrible dilemma of what is right and what is wrong but to fight his kinsfolk as that was the only way to righteousness. Ultimately, Pandavas won the Mahabharata war at the end of the 18th day and Yudhisthira, the eldest of Pandava brothers, was crowned the king of Hastinapur.

The *Mahabharata,* written by Veda Vyas, is a colossal work, an encyclopedia of tradition and legend, of political and social institutions of ancient India. A very definite attempt has been made in the grand epic to emphasize the fundamental unity of India - a unity of outlook among the people which was to survive and overshadow all diversity. *Mahabharata* also lays stress on ethical and moral principles in statecraft, and in life in general. The aim is social welfare, not the welfare of a particular group only, but of the whole world. For, it says, "the entire world of mortals is a self-dependent organism." *Mahabharata* also contains the legends of Krishna and the famous poem, *Bhagavad Gita.* It is accepted as the most beautiful philosophical song existing in any human tongue anywhere in the world. It is a poem of crisis, of political and social crisis and, even more so, of crisis in the spirit of man, which, from age to age, has been torn by the conflict of duties, obligations and moralities. Here, from a personal conversation, between Arjuna and Krishna on the field of battle, we are taken step by step to higher and more impersonal regions of individual duty and social behaviour, of the application of ethics to human life, of the spiritual outlook that should govern all. The message of the *Gita* is not at all sectarian or addressed to any particular school of thought; it is universal in its approach and, for that reason, had found favour with all. There is something in it that seems to be eternally capable of being constantly renewed, which does not become out of date with the passage of time. That something is an inner quality, the quality of earnest inquiry and search, of contemplation and action, of balance and equilibrium in spite of conflict and contradiction.

Dinkar, the eminent Hindi poet who was also hailed as *Rashtrakavi* (national poet) in his time, wrote *Kurukshetra* on the above-mentioned themes of *Mahabharata.* This poem of epic proportions, known for its elegance and musical rhythm, is in a sense a re-reinterpretation of the nuances of thought as ensconced in its classical theme. It was in this context that the poet was drawn towards the character of Yudhisthira, the eldest of Pandava brothers. As depicted in *Kurukshetra*, toward the end of the Mahabharata war, this rightful heir-apparent of the dynasty of Kuru kings seemed to be weighing victory against the dead bodies. Yet indeed, here, too, in Kurukshetra, the main theatre of the Mahabharata war, in the utterances of Bhisma - the eldest of the Kurus - lay another aspect of the problem. The battle of soul (the internal dilemma) is won by the soul itself, and the battle of body (external preoccupations) is won by the body. The poet, in *Kurukshetra,* thus deals with the aftermath of the Mahabharata war. The essence of what Lord Krishna had spoken to Arjuna (*Gita*) at the inception of thc battle was "the negation of exhibition of austerity in opposition to injustice and inequity".

War is condemnable, a cruel act in itself; but upon whom should lie the responsibility of its initiation? Should it lie upon him who invites retaliation by spreading a web of injustice and inequities? Or should it lie upon him who is bound by oath to sever the net of war asunder? Duryodhana, the Kaurava prince, had imposed an uneasy reign of peace by banishing the Pandavas out of the kingdom of Hastinapur. The question that arose was whether it was unethical and unreasonable on the part of Yudhisthira to break that uneasy peace for the sake of justice? These were the issues which Dinkar ponders over in *Kurukshetra* all through its seven cantos. In the rendition of the characters of Bhisma and Yudhisthira the poet has put these ethical issues in perspective by dwelling upon the eternal problem of war and peace, as he could comprehend it. It is for this reason Dinkar admits that Bhisma and Yudhisthira of his *Kurukshetra* are not the exact replicas of Bhisma and Yudhisthira of Veda Vyas' *Mahabharata.* Although the poet has consciously avoided any anachronism in the meaningful dialogues uttered by Bhisma and Yudhisthira, he has been at liberty to adapt the statements of Bhisma to the tune of our times and has dwelt upon them in a new light and from an angle conducive to modern-day thought. At times, the poet has visualized the answers Bhisma would have given for the problems that are akin to the issues in discussion. It is at these junctures in *Kurukshetra* that the poet's genius finds full consummation. Moreover, the poet is truthful enough to take responsibility for the aberrations in the flight of his imagination, for the thoughts and actions that are not in conformity with the themes and thoughts of the Dwapar age. In fact, the whole of Canto VI belongs to this genre, a genre which can survive as an independent poem if plucked off from the *Kurukshetra* corpus.

Dinkar's poetry, while emanating in the form of dialogues from the quivering lips of the arrow-ridden Bhisma, gets lost in the sublimity of thoughts; and yet the poet himself opines that his *Kurukshetra* is neither a treatise on philosophy nor a miracle of the mature mind of a wise man. For Dinkar, it is his ever-doubting heart that has embarked upon the job of thinking. Dinkar's interpretation of Bhisma is strikingly modern. The suggestion that Bhisma fell not by Arjuna's arrows, but as a voluntary victim to the upsurge of his long-repressed tender emotions, is daringly novel and, from the viewpoint of modern psychology, quite plausible. As the invincible patriarch lies supine in the battle-field perched on the bed of arrows, shot from Arjuna's mighty bow, awaiting the final moment, the terror of being judged sharpens his memory and sends an inevitable glare over that long unvisited part which he has never recalled. With memory set smarting like a reopened wound, Bhisma's past is not simply a dead history, an outworn preparation of the present : it is not a repented error shaken loose from the life : it is still a quivering part of himself, bringing shudders and bitter flavours and the tinglings of a merited or unmerited shame.

The apotheosis, or the tipping point, of the epic is reached in the seventh canto where in beautifully rhymed stanzas and deftly-controlled cadences as well as through pictorial metaphors Dinkar conveys his own moral wisdom through Bhisma, who strips bare the poet's own mind. In fact, Canto VII of this meditative epic will undoubtedly survive all ravages of time, transcend all limits of space, and inspire all human hearts, of the dim and distant lands, as well as of the generations to come, as we are reminded of a Shakespearean sonnet:

So long as men can breathe, or eyes can see,
So long lives this, and this gives life to thee.

Dr. Shachi Kant **Dr. Raman P. Singh**

Contents

Corrigendum Page

The publishers regret the following printing errors in the book. Bold-lettered words denote corrections:

p. 22 first para: Separate paragraph should start from the line *Ere the outbreak of war*

p.22 first para: *A ontend* should be read as **contend**

p.23 second para 1st line; the line should read: **And when the thunderous**

p.33 fifth para, 2nd line: remove "the" in the line. The line will now read like this: **Aware, too, of its aftermath**

p.41 third para of Canto III, 4th line; remove *with* before *peace*, replace with **let**. The line should read: **let peace be your only intent**.

p.46 remove note of exclamation (!) in first para in 2nd line

p.46 remove comma (,) after *Or* in fourth para in 2nd line

p.49 first para in 2nd line. Give space in the word *cardinalsin*. The line will now read as **cardinal sin**.

p.120 first para, 2nd line. Replace capital *E* of *Eever* by capital **N**. The word will now read as **Never**

Corrigendum Page

CANTO - I

Who is that yonder wails,
In history's tattered tales?
Wherein it's large writ that the worth of youths' blood
Is nothing but the guile of some wily old wizard's word,
Whose loveless heart is as dark as his hairline is white,
Who, being wise, never embarks himself on a fatal fight;
Yet makes sacrifices of young lives to show his might:
Thinks then, at ease, assured of the feat of his brave deed,
"The land's honour is saved, no matter if our kindred bleed".

And then with due veneration do we reminisce
Those men whose brides lost their marital bliss
For keeping aglow the radiant face of the country;
Or, those mothers who their dear sons forever miss,
Who gave their lives to save the multitudinous gentry.

God knows whether the moot point of national dignity,
Forsooth, is a bare appearance or some tangible reality,
Of that venomous, tortuous fire of rancour and spite
Which has been simmering since all bygone years;
Like the all-consuming famished fires burning bright
In the bellies of a kingdom's self-covetous pioneers.

A cosmopolite's unmalicious heart and head
Can never in the furnace of hate be rooted;
No community does ever by itself war covet,

In the breath of evil men the flames of war do spread.
Ere the outbreak of war, incertitude does with growing ire A ontend,
Ere the onset of each war, man ponders whether only arms portend
The proven anodyne as well as an unerring remedy
For poison, dishonour, venomous hate 'n' inequity.

Man must fight his best,
Yet after the conquest,
He beholds, on the battlefield, how truth fails,
The truth that weeps in history's tattered tales,
Drenching the deeds of the victor with tearful wails.

Truth's shuddering impact does sting,
Stirring the still and listless veins,
Like unknown fingers strumming the string,
Writhes in helpless pain spread in the veins,
Knows well that there can be no healing.

Of a sudden, surging from the heart, does emanate
The irreversible arrow of truth, and thus reverberate;
"What have I done, O Lord! With man's blood I'm wet".
But man's spirit, perchance, of stone is made;
Forgetting soon the sting and bite of past pain,
Once more the dreaded path of war does he tread,
Once more his brethren he slays, himself in turn is slain.
Yet after the conquest, again, vain tears does he shed.

So it happened, long ago in the battle of the Kuru(1) clan,
When the macabre dance of death was reaching its close;
Having vengefully drunk the blood from the breast of a man,
When the wrathful Bhîma(2) was in the grip of anger's throes;

And when open-haired Draupadi(3), from her oath unbound,
Had kept ablaze the flame of vengeance until she found
A vent for revenge, gnashed her teeth in wrathful throes;
Smearing her hair with the hot blood of her sworn foes,

She did into a serpentine plait braid her abundant tresses,
Those for thirteen torpid years were *sans* locks 'n' caresses.

And when the thunderous Pandava Bhima, at his best,
The jewel from the forehead of Drona's[4] son did wrest
And, joyously, the trophy bestowed to his beloved one,
As if it were a prize from the Pandavas, who had won.

To offer the last oblations to Kauravas'[5] ashes
Or to mourn at the pyres their ruinous losses,
When of the remaining kinsfolk there were none,
Save Dhritrashtra[6], the blind king, and a crone.

And, when, wafting aloft from the Pandavas'[7] camp,
The shrill notes of jubilation, bearing victory's stamp,
Meandering pathless on the sepulchral field of battle,
Wobbling on the wind, did like a roaring voice rattle;
Yet turning its stray course back to whence it came,
Vented on the listening ears victory's enduring fame
As though mocking them for their brazen shame:
"Behold yonder, the reign of lull after the dreaded doom
Gone are they all, to whom my presence spelt gloom."

The tell-tale scorn, in the roar of conquest inherent,
The scorn hidden in jubilation, who can discern or bear?
When one and all are fully spent in joyous content,
The thrill of victory has caused their senses to disappear.

But amid the victorious, delirious ensemble,
There's a man who's listless but atremble,
Not a sigh does he heave; with arrows pierced,
But wails inwardly, in deep thought immersed:

"Far away from tumult, envy and fear,
Indeed, they all are long way gone;
But the dead never come back to hear,

The rejoicing is but the victor's scorn."

As though in a phantasma, thus spake Suyodhana [8];
"O Yudhisthira[9]! We've sailed beyond life's ocean;
Whatever evil ignominies you might upon us heap,
Are of very little worth in our posthumous sleep;

We are yonder where the battle prime
Appears like a fathomless abyss of fantasy;
One that seems to have occurred sometime;
Yet whose meaning is lost to the memory;

We've come across, you're yonder in quest,
Pray, speak, whose loss is it, whose victory?
Do savour now the trophies of your conquest,
Of penance, agony's torment and mockery."

The sound of jubilation, wandering in the battle-field,
Staggered aimlessly and did then to utter silence yield.
Yet Yudhisthira hearkened the sound of that phantasmal voice
Emanating from his heart's tumult or from the pervading void:

"The battle-field, soaked in blood, made
Twain miles of deep earth crimson red;
And aloft the waves of gushing blood-stream
Mangled limbs of steeds 'n' elephants swim.

"Yet after this annihilation and waste,
What remains but Fate's mocking disdain;
The truth that I did aspire to wrest,
Has it to fruition come, or is it in vain?

"In sooth, along with my adversaries, the end
That I did yearn to ultimately comprehend,
Has all but vanished, in my hands leaving,
Only scorn, rancour, remorse and grieving;

"The battle has ended, leaving others to mourn,
Ah! How fiercely ablaze is the venomous scorn?
The malice of revenge that five men had sought,
Has to ruins and ashes the whole land brought;

"To drape and garb Draupadi in radiant dress
And for us to relish this denuded kingdom,
Countless wives and mothers became kinless
Their husbands 'n' sons lost to vain martyrdom;

"How can I lord over this truncated 'n' ruined empire,
Drenched in blood? Methinks of stone I would turn;
Smeared and splattered, as it is, with the bloody mire
Of humans, where Abhimanyu's [(10)] gore yet does churn."

As though a thunderclap did crash from the memory's crust,
One that stamped Yudhisthira down with its onerous thrust;
With this, his thirsting and craving intellect was fain to speak,
A mind that yet amidst the battle's ashes some truth did seek.

With grief and agony was the heart so filled,
Whence neither foam nor froth ever spilled;
Yet heaving a sigh of unquiet torment, he said,
"O Parth[(11)]! To Pitamaha[(12)] for counsel do I tread."

And the roar of rejoicing, ringing in the void
Did stagger and wobble on the wind and died.

CANTO - II

"Ye know", said Bhisma the Invincible without any misgiving,
To Death's looming spectre, "the propitious moment of my leaving
Has yet not arrived, so stay awhile"; uttering thus, he lay supine
On the bed of arrows, his head on the prop of arrows did recline.
Vyas (1) narrates, he lay thus sprawled, unfettered, unbound,
Having wrenched from Death his life breath, while around
Somewhere in a nearby nook, Death lay meekly in wait,
Hands enfolded, as she stood in obedience to his *diktat*.

As though surveying across his life, from aloft a high brim
Engrossed in deep meditation lay Pitamaha, pensive 'n' grim.
And Dharmaraja(2) saw the sprightly and glimmering flame,
Radiating from his white mien and his arrow-nailed frame.
Paying obeisance, touching with head the revered feet,
Washing the toes with cascading streams of tears sweet,
Lamented Dharmaraja in grief, as if impatient 'n' restless,
"Ah! Pitamaha, the Mahabharata war is rendered fruitless.

"Suyodhana's flown, astride the wings of martyrdom's fame
Leaving in my frail, sagging arms, his stiff and lifeless frame,
And before me, the sight of colossal stretch of ruin 'n' waste;
As if blaring in the sky the clarion of his posthumous conquest;
And this mortal shape that now remains,
As if speaks quietly, in hushing silence–
"Pray, speak, I'm victory's sole trophy,
Whose triumph is it? Whose catastrophe?"

"Ah! Pitamaha, whose defeat eventually is it?
Who does his head on the vestiges of ravages beat?
Who does vain pleasure seek in the ashes and ruins?
Who with flames of fire the raiment of diadem spins?
And, seated on the shore of a human blood stream,
Who ponders over the scornful import of fate's whim?
Who does the cremation of kinsfolk behold to bear?
Who does the heart-rending wail of Uttara (3) hear?

"If to me was foreknown the gory aftermath of the royal battle,
Giving up prowess, with moral strength I'd choose to grapple,
Conquering with sufferance 'n' abnegation Suyodhana's head,
The firm foundation of a bright new annals I would have laid;
And if, perchance, my sighs hadn't the silent stone broken,
If my penance the cruel heart of Suyodhana had not woken;
Even so, alas! I would not have let this blood-bath occur,
Along with my dear brethren I'd go a-begging for succour.

"But, ah! The very day the seeds of the battle were sown,
My perception and wisdom did not quite with me bear;
The thunderous club of Bhima sieged my intellect, and won
Me over, as did the great bow of Parth and my own spear;
And when illusion ensnared Arjuna before the onset of battle,
To the smouldering 'n' billowing fire did Krishna(4) add fuel;
Ah! The good sense, Pitamaha, of one and all vanished,
For their flamboyance and vainglory all were demolished.

"Krishna preaches, *the act of war is bereft of sin*,
But my spirit flares up in remorse on the loss of kin,
Methinks! Why cannot man, crown of the universe,
Save himself from this incendiary, ancient curse?
And all talk of gallantry in battle is vain 'n' *sans* vision,
When great heroes like you were felled by treason,
The slaughter of Abhimanyu and Suyodhana portend,
That none amongst us remained from sins unstained.

"At one end is the Lord's truth, as in the *Gita* [5] enshrined,
On the other, disenchantment from life is clearly defined;
Methinks! I had waged the battle for justice's ultimate sake,
Yet this blood-spangled conquest forever seems to me fake;
Doom-begetting mirth, or the teary peace-bearing gloom,
Which of the twain is against ethics, is to me yet unknown;
Methinks! I'm unaware if, on Kurukshetra[6], virtue did bloom,
Or some dreadful vice, in the form of this battle, has grown.

"In the coronet of the Kuru clan, so easily gotten,
Lies concealed a fierce, fiery, inflammable flare;
Will coronation purge my heart that's with sin sodden?
For sinners, the holy water is a potion bringing despair;
Victory, like a frightful she-cobra, stings my mind,
To cope with which I have neither strength nor fire;
How can I accept; for, time 'n' again, do I ever find
The royal pleasures like lotuses in blood-filled mire.

"Sometimes the dismal bemoaning of son-bereaved mothers rend the air,
At other moments, the dolorous wails of orphaned babes are heard there;
Lo and behold! Wherever I look, ah! There I behold the loss of coverture,
The sight of wiped vermilion marks that bridal foreheads did once nurture;
When, from outdoors, I seek refuge in my abode's innermost recesses,
Therein, I hear too the resounding thunder of Time's scornful curses;
Whether wakeful, or asleep, I come to sudden fits and dream,
Methinks! I heard the blood of Abhimanyu oozing a scream.

"Since the fires of battle, dying-out, were doused,
A solitary flame still remained ablaze and aroused;
Ah! Pitamaha, I find my deeds so vain and without fame,
That I can scarce my countenance uphold to this shame;
It seems as though people stare at me in horrible disgust,
Cries of eternal perdition do I hear in every speck of dust;
On seeing fellow humans, my eyes evade to see, in shame
The desire to flee to woods creeps stealingly over my frame.

"The slur will be more damning if I choose to die by suicide,
So, leaving this dwelling, in a sylvan retreat I'll my time abide;
There streams of tears will I shed, concealed in a cavern,
Where the eyes of neither beast nor bird could ever discern;
Though I'm aware my sins won't be cleansed by hermitage,
Yet forgetting my grief there I'll hide in my self-created cage
Where scorn, ever anew, won't let my weary heart be blown,
There, in the woods, I'll not again as Dharmaraja be known."

Restraining somehow his boundless torment,
Kaunteya [7], thence, became grim and silent,
Like the vast and rimless clouds without end
Laden with rain, yet sodden with constraint,
From pouring down, restless but contained.

Then Bhisma [8] stirred, looked skyward, as if divining
The depth of Yudhisthira's heart's brimful whining;
"Ah! Ye, the model of humans," he sighed, grieving:
"Will ye ever cross the darkness of this fateful night,
Wake up in the rare realm of the Truth's ideal light,
That's come to shape now in the life of this celibate,
From the lethal blows of renouncement and regret?"

To Yudhisthira, then he said, "have you ever seen a tempest,
How like the thunder it comes, striding the blast of calamity;
Like the devil jerking and splitting the trees in the deep forest,
Uprooting in wrath, and rolling aground with fierce depravity,
Those thousand plants that are feebly embedded in earth's cavity,
How, with a cracking, scary sound, the emaciated boughs do break,
As the nests of fowls, with their young, tumbling, to the ground take,
With broken trees and twigs replete, the spectre of Nature distends,
Bedecked with scattered bunches of flowers and dead birds she bends.

But the mammoth tree, its roots deep in the depths of earth spread,
Scarce ever takes fright at the cruel onslaught of the terrible tempest.
The tumultuous hurricane blows down, rustling past its lofty head,

Plucking some leaves, wrenching a few branches in its hurried haste.
Yet whatever remains, surviving in the wake of the stormy boom,
Like the loss of sylvan riches and the plight of the dowager trees,
These the live, mammoth tree beholds, in detachment and gloom,
Drooping low its listless leaves looks to the heavens in unease,
And thinks, "Ah! Why does Nature send us the fury of the doom?"

But the inanimate tree scarcely knows,
Nature too is bound by the laws of motion,
This furious hurricane is not for her foes;
But, it's her spirit's impulsive explosion,
Accumulating from fierce heat, and impetuous,
Its eruption is necessary, though tempestuous.

So, too, within fiery forms of perversities men get embroiled,
Merging in each other, flaring up with force, up they coiled,
Igniting the inner horizons of many men, their senses foiled,
And then, the societal order bursts into fiery conflagration,
Fuelled by abhorrence, envy, malice, venom and dejection.
When patterns are formed of such devious trends,
The volcano of war erupts thence, and distends,
Either on the pretext of some political need,
Or pepped up by patriotism's flaming creed.

But such-like poisons are in war's varied origins laid,
That, endemic-like, from rancour and disgust spread.

One and all, ever and anon, are aware of war's bane,
Aware, too, of the its aftermath, which is ever in vain;
Ah! To slaughter millions for the rejoicing of five brethren!

But, pray, don't surmise, that in the battle of the Kuru plain,
The happiness of the Pandavas alone was in pre-eminence;
For what, in sooth, mattered to those in the battle slain,
Not the pains 'n' perils of the five, but the ethical sense.

In their hearts lay ensconced many an emotional desire,
Of flaming valour, manhood, or selfish ambition's fire;
The spasms which propelled them into the battle's fire,
Had other roots, too, springing from the upsurge of ire.

The hysterics of war are so terribly inflammable,
No sooner is a single spark ignited, it does enable
Unleashing of tidal gusts of wind that are ungovernable,
Consumed by fire, billowing with many a fiery bubble.

But does war's terrible spectre leave an outlet
For meditation on self, with ponderings replete?
The flames of battle throw down the gauntlet
To the tiger, hidden deep in the human spirit.

Harking the cry of challenge, vengeance dares,
Cautions pride, whose torrid swell spurts flares,
The blood yearns to burst the veins and drip
And the sword, of itself, comes in the fist's grip.

No one ever craves the eruption of a malady,
But when the disease afflicts all in its spread,
What else is better than a pungent remedy?
For it will scarce by sweetmeats be allayed.

The rattle of your heavy heart is in vain,
That thinks of war as virtue or misdeed;
For there is, in very sooth, no such deed
Which in itself is evil or good in its strain.

Lord Krishna spake the truth, when he explained,
"What matters is the belief of the doer's heart,
And the crucial idea is - how detached we remained
From our actions, in the battle of life, how apart."

And war, all the more, is an exception,

An event none yearns for with volition;
Yet, one and all have to bear and contend
When the foe strikes us to ours' wits' end.

Enough, upto now, I have heard and observed,
But the riddle of virtue 'n' vice stays unresolved;
The truth is, no line I can demarcate 'n' divide,
Betwixt what's good or what's bad in its stride.

I am aware too that to live through life,
A flame of valour is surely required;
War can scarce ever be evil, if it springs
From the spirit of a vengeance, that stings.

It's a sin to practise austerity and not fight,
When you're being deprived of your right;
A virtue it is to mangle and to sever to pieces,
The hand that toward you menacingly reaches.

The bound, broken and the bootless
Have but the right prop of their curses;
But why should a man's sinewy arms
Beseech humble entreaties, or beg alms?

You hold that the act of war is condemnable,
But so long as the sparks remain distinguishable
Of our divergent self-interests that are unassailable;
Until then, the occurrence of war is indispensable.

It's vain and dross to be despondent and dejected,
For that which is destined and cannot be resisted;
Whether or not you had waged war in any context,
It was bound to break out on any pettifogging pretext.

This burst of hostilities would scarce have ceased,
Even if the Pandavas had with beggary been pleased.

For, many an ominous star conspired in wrath to beget
War, being hell-bent on unleashing doom upon the planet.

There is one more hidden secret of faith,
Why should I conceal it now from futurity?
A few days I'll hold good on the crest of death,
Then I, too, will tread the way of all mortality.

The faith of man abounds in compassion, mercy, and austerity,
The true grace of man is manifested in humility and abnegation;
But when the issue is not of Self but of the community,
We've to put aside and ignore austerity and renunciation.

The spirit of universal mercy, abiding in your heart in plenty,
Alone weeps and wails over the Kauravas' benighted calamity.
But, pray, ask that spirit, imbued with collective emotions aplenty,
Whether the gory battle of Mahabharata was not a necessity?

When the Pandavas set out for beggardom, losing hearth 'n' prosperity,
Then, pray, ask, how this flagrant act was betaken by their community,
Which was an ally of the Pandavas and was to the hilt opposed to inequity.

And when like a virtuous man in dilemma, having lost
All, beheld like a eunuch, your consort being disrobed;
(As with Draupadi, the dignity of the community as host
Too was trampled, that had come under Pandavas' fold);
Ye did not take any remedial action, had nothing to boast;
Was it virtue? Or, virtuous was that dreadful, impetuous ire,
Which had flared up, in the eyes of Bhima, like a furious fire?

•

Don't singe and scorch me with your coward-like twaddle,
Unto this day sacrifice and valour have ever been my ideal;
Having lit the torch of heroism in the community's temple,
I would depart from this world, astride the wings of battle.

Abnegation, austerity, alms? I too know enough and more of such ethics,
But abnegation, austerity and alms fashion the faith of detached ascetics;
Such ideas mark the traits of men, without bows 'n' arrows in hand;
Or, perchance, are the false pretences of impotent cowards' band,
Who are, ever and now, scared of battle, all the time thinking
That a life of ignominy is better, while death is undeserving.
Imbued with abnegation, austerity, mercy, and compassion,
The heart of an individual burns bright with throbbing passion;
But, when, ferocious beasts of prey surround him and yelp,
It's the virile human body that comes to his instant help.

And that which you call the inward moral force,
Can scarce be the weapon of physical resource;
Its real abode is that luminous psychic entity,
Wherein man contends with his perversity.
Who can ever succeed in physical battles,
If by spiritual vigour alone he grapples.
When bestiality raises its awful sword,
Moral strength finds the end of the road.

The inner strength, innate in austerity and in sacrifice,
Only in an individual's heart finds regards that suffice;
The power of ascetics in this mundane, earthly universe,
Can scarce ever render the defeat of a host so enormous.

When Rama[9], having seen in the forest the heap of hermits' bones,
Took a solemn pledge to slaughter the horrible and devilish demons;
The tender-hearted Sita[10] had, thence, posed the wisest of questions,
'Is arms the proven anodyne for redemption of deranged humans?'
Rama, thence, had observed, being the noblest of all the humans,
'No dear, man can be reformed by austerities, too, and abnegations;
But austerity cannot forever suffice, nor the bare pursuit of piety,
When accosted by the malignant instincts of a fallen community.'

CANTO - III

War's condemnable, ye know, O Dharmaraja!
But, pray, speak, what's that elusive peace
Which, founded on inequity's camouflage,
Poses just and artless yet, remains at ease?
Garnering up a boundless and multitudinous repository
Of pleasure 'n' prosperity, by force, deceit 'n' cunning;
Snatching tiny morsels from the famished, the hungry;
Plundering the wealth of many a hapless weakling;

She thus gathers all and posts a sentinel on guard,
Bids each and everyone, 'don't ye speak a word'
She says, 'the elixir of peace is gently afloat,
Don't dare dissolve into it the venom of revolt.

Don't ye ever quake or quiver with unease,
Let me drink your life-blood to heart's content;
Enduring and firm be the reign of such peace,
Live and let live, with peace be your only intent.

It's true, forsooth, that as power passes over,
Slowly into the hands of those who are clever,
Who pretend to be devotees of peaceful ease,
Why, at all, would they desire battle and unease?

Where the equitable dispersal of prosperity
Is not rendered through justice and equity,

Where the spectre of unease and unrest
Is crushed underneath by the sword's thrust;

Where the vile system of inequity
Is nurtured by powerful potentates,
Where the saviors of the society
Are but its tyrants and hot-heads;

Where judicious proposals of treaty
Aren't met with a cordial reception,
Where intrepid speakers of reality
Are beheaded as a stark convention;

Where the power of scimitar
Is the system's sole arbiter,
Where the hearts of oppressed
Are ablaze with ire repressed;

Where the mind of man is forever dying, ever in distress,
Bearing forever and more the onerous brunt of injustice,
Where people are crying themselves hoarse with curses,
Where everyone is swearing shameful cowardice;

Where the contending duel of intense hate
With vainglorious vanity is forever on fret,
Where peace glitters brightly upon the surface,
But discontent swirls menacingly in the depths;

Where the spectre of imminent explosions
Upon the wearied face of Time simmers;
Where blazing embers of impotent emotions
Portend awesome, fretful looming gestures;

Where the potentates and the wielders of fiat
Are unaware of the tell-tale signs of disquiet;
Where time and again, by turns, they ignite
The all-consuming fires of evil-some sprite;

Oft, and betimes, they proffer a new game,
Of newer extortions, negligence and shame,
Sometimes, too, they give offerings of disgrace,
And, oft, they pour disdainful words face to face;

If the smouldering passions would embroil
There, and burst forth in a terrible turmoil;
If man, forsaking restraint, would then assail
His vile tormentors like the fury of the gale;

O Yudhisthira! Who shall be responsible
For the genocidal conflagration, so horrible?
Which of the twain, hate or vanity, shall be guilty
Of waging the battle? Who shall take responsibility?

Ye're despondent because ye ponder,
That your hands set the world on fire.
But, think, did the fire of battle-cry
Fall on the earth from the high sky?

Or, did the flames of war flare upwards,
All of a sudden from the earth's innards,
Or, were the flames begotten of the sacrificial altars,
Consecrated with *mantras*, with their great powers.

Wasn't the battle royale already astir,
Ere the onset of the Kurukshetra War?
Wasn't the vengeful flame of hatred, of yore,
Set fiercely ablaze in all hearts, from before?

When peace unsheathes her dazzling sword
To cry revolt against the oppressive hoard,
Know thou! It's then that the seeds are sown
And the lines of a dreadful battle are drawn.

Peace can't reign supreme unless the share
Of human happiness be fair and square,

None should have too much 'n' more,
None else too little for his own score.

Such a benevolent peace forever reigns
Over human love, respect, and reverence,
Over the high-soaring beliefs of everyman,
Over the bosom, but not the body of man,

Justice is the very corner-stone of peace,
Until it falls, broken into many a piece;
The castle of peace, though indefatigable;
Can scarcely be labelled insurmountable.

Imposed peace, ever in diffidence,
Doubts and fears her own spectre,
And scarcely reposes confidence
In anyone except her own sabre.

And who to happiness,
Has such an easy access,
For him peace is the essence of life;
An ideal for which forever to strive.

But by gnawing whose bones and marrow,
By sucking whose life blood *sans* sorrow,
Lives this peace, and what it aspires to?
Consider their unappeasable agony, too!

When the rights of man are not by beseeching granted,
When opposing evil becomes a reprehensible, sinful act;
O Dharmaraja! Say, whether the oppressed and exploited
Of this world should live or die? Pray, speak truly the fact.

When fair 'n' equal rights are not bestowed
By making vain entreaties to the proud,
Then, the valiant wrests them in the battle,
Or dies while performing an act that is fatal.

Who said it is evil to struggle and to fight
For the acquisition of the just rights of men?
Is't evil to raise the sword of justice 'n' fight
Bravely in the battle, and to slay, or be slain?

By making vain pleas in the name, often
Of deserved merit, mercy 'n' compassion,
O Dharmaraja! Don't ye seem more often
To suggest the cowardice inherent in man?

When and where has meditation borne
The crushing stroke of brutal, devilish force?
The ensemble of gods finding no recourse,
Had been losing battles to many a demon.

If your inward strength was more dear
Than the blaze of your manly vigour,
Why did ye Bharat's [(1)] kingdom covet?
Why did ye, at all, return from the forest?

Bhima drank the lethal potion [(2)] and the shellac-house [(3)] was burnt,
Thence to the woods were the Pandavas exiled from kingdom's front,
Disheveled, ragged and unfurled were their spouse's lovely tresses,
As she was shamed by the assembled folks and their wanton passes.

Mercy, morale, meditation, sacrifice 'n' compassion,
Of all these, and more, did you take ready succour?
But, say, when or where did the devilish Suyodhana
Lose to you ever during the whole damned affair?

Tolerant, laden full with the sap of mercy,
Humbler ye behaved with the adversary;
The meek, weak, and more of a game,
To the wicked Kauravas you became.

This is verily the unhappy consequence

Of bearing atrocities in a long sequence,
Thus do men, becoming soft 'n' tender!
Lose the fire and dread of manly vigour.

Pardon behoves that hissing serpent,
Whose terrible fangs do venom vent;
Forgiveness doesn't behove those who're humble,
Toothless and non-venomous, they only grumble.

Upon the coast of the Ocean, for three days on end,
Raghupati (4) made entreaties for a path to the island,
Reciting awhile sweet rhymes in prayful posture,
Rapt in supplication, he lay still in gentle gesture.

When, in response, not even a single sound,
Or, hum emanated from the ocean unbound,
Rama's arrows flared up, in all readiness,
Betokening the raging fire of manliness.

The still Ocean, manifesting itself in the human shape,
Came tumbling down for refuge, begging cries of help,
Worshipping his feet, the sea-god prostrated to Rama,
And, like a fool, was fettered to the command of Rama.

Verily, on the tip of the arrowhead,
Dwells the splendour of humility;
His pledge of treaty is venerated,
Who has the sinews for victory.

Mercy, compassion and tolerance;
In this world are held in reverence,
When force abetted by arrogance
Glows 'n' sparkles brightly whence.

Where the power of redemption is amiss,
In vain are the protestations of mercy.

To drink the lethal draught is no bliss,
It's merely the tongue's vile duplicity.

Those who conceal their timid cowardices,
Wrapping it in the blanket of forgivenesses
Pray! How would they know of spirit's fortitude,
Of the virile man's dependence on his manhood?

They can scarce know of that hidden,
Suppressed fire in the human vein,
Which, with a mere touch, is goaded,
Surging up from the heart to the head.

The sinewy nerve of whose arms never strains,
Whose blood lacks the gusts of fire in its veins,
The dregs of altars have ever been whose succour,
Whose tongues did never savour poison's ardour;
In whose hearts no sparks ever leapt into flames,
Whose pride, before licking their wounds, spilt,
Who have not the buffer of vigour in their arms,
They alone confide in the strength of the spirit.

What's the purpose of his endurance and mercy,
Who knows not how to strike the awful blows?
What other means remain, save pardon and pity,
For him who cannot wreak vengeance on his foes?
Only the helpless and timid creature bears assault,
In whose veins the stream of prowess barely flows,
Pity 'n' mercy are the stark stains of a eunuch's lot,
The capacity for forgiveness is the jewel of heroes.

The flames of valour are, by vengeance, made luminous,
While revengelessness among men is a vice ignominious;
Relinquishing hostility's return, they alone swallow disgrace,
In whom the sparks of bravery's fire have no radiant glow;
Suffering injury and hurt, how can he wear endurance's face,

Whose quiver has arrows, whose hand wields the firm bow?
Forbearance and forgiveness are the ornaments of the victors,
But to the lot of the vanquished, forgiveness becomes a curse.

Whithersoever one single straw dares touch its body,
The serpent spits its venomous hiss in terrible frenzy;
As in woods the elephant blares its trumpet sound,
And the lion, from its lair, roars a thunderous sound;
The spear hurts, and, with its touch, the fire burns,
Lo! To swallow earth, the ocean thunders, as it churns;
The glory of these sparkles in the world, as they strike,
Revenge is the birth-right of animate 'n' inanimate alike.

To wield power to frighten and usurp another's right,
To fight for avarice does not behove a gallant's might,
Virtue is never born of carnal objects; it's unrighteous,
The sword, dangling in a merchant's hand, is impious.
But the lion, when wounded, wakes up from slumber,
Vengeance, wide awake, seethes with dreadful anger;
The virtue shines in the glitter of the sword's blade,
And the upsurgence of manhood is named crusade.

The attribute of fire is to burst forth in blazes, of course,
Why does anyone summon a wind of momentous force?
The fierce mouths of dormant volcanoes would fain erupt,
The lambent earth would yawn her craters to raise tumult?
The serpent, by its very hiss, will surely the earth scorch,
Why would anyone prod it up with a pearly prickly touch?
Lightening from the celestial sphere would descend surely,
Why would anyone kick off and hurt the fiery pride vainly?

Who does summon war? The flag-bearer of inequity,
Or him that strides on the forehead of impropriety?
He that is weighed down under extortions weighty,
Or him that stands ecstatic, rollicking with laughter?
He that, devising an array of peace, revels in pleasure,
Or him that famishes with the fire of iniquitous hunger?

Who summons up war? He that springs up the dragnet,
Or him that emerges, furious as Death, to sever the net?

The swords of the wakeful but oppressed are not steeped in sin
To speak of it as sinful is an error of philosophy, a cardinalsin,
A peace that's founded on a system of extortion, as in monarchy,
Is, in fact, a war; it's verily, too, a mute but terrifying anarchy;
To suffer it in quietude is truly the veritable defeat of humanity,
It's a disregard to God, and the loss of manhood's real strength;
It's the vice in man, and the demise of all the good in humanity,
In such an order, revolution and revolt comprise the true faith.

O Dharmaraja! Ye seem to forget,
That the planet earth is violent yet,
Vanity stands aloft on every side,
And deceit is rampant in its tide.

I too often times ponder the ways,
To remove from world atrocity,
To spread the gospel, in this Age,
Of love, non-violence, and piety.

How men would live in cool compatibility,
Being each other's brethren in reciprocity;
How the conflagration of ire would ease,
How the strife would, perchance, cease.

Let the earth be love's wide kingdom,
Let life be simple, bereft of stratagem,
Let all the fiery rancour and venom
Soon depart from human genome.

Let the stream of love go ever with the flow,
Drenching mankind in its incessant outflow,
And all men, in each other's hearts, to sow
The seeds of love that forever would grow.

But alas! The universe and its people
Have traversed only half their journey,
As yet, the dream of a peace tranquil
Glitters brightly in some distant galaxy.

That ideal light descends but rarely on earth,
As though it had strayed away from its course,
And, then, such as in Yudhisthira's life-breath,
It gradually forms its bright 'n' radiant contours.

But crashing oft and betimes,
On the rocky citadel of Time,
Finding at once the grim iron-door,
Of mankind's thwarted mental shore,

Distressed by many a diverse affliction,
Such as bickering, hatred, and rancour,
That nectar of peace vanishes into thin air,
Drenching rarely the heart of any person.

For there is indeed but one Yudhisthira only,
While very many Suyodhanas roam fiercely,
Alas! Where is the life-giving, nurturing sap,
For the peace-vines to grow and bridge the gap.

The flute of peace scarcely rings
In clear, definite notes, and sings,
Unless the pure resonance of tones
Don't zing in all the hearts 'n' bones.

It's not indeed an outward instrument,
That alights from above like a burden,
It's the light of the soul that gives vent,
Ever to the immaculate inward terrain.

Peace is the name of that pleasant cascade,

With which the spirit of love does associate,
Whose sway, not only the ferocious sword,
But the heart of mankind also does hold.

The images 'n' idols of beneficent peace
Are not carved in the sculptor's niche,
It's ever bred, conceived, and begotten,
In the selfless realm of the human ken.

Precluding, with success, the germination
Of venom, malice, animus, and eruption,
The ardent human nature transforms
Itself into serene and tranquil forms.

When this peace becomes incarnate,
Nothing remains of any fear or fret,
No single realm remains under clout
Of the benighted darkness of doubt.

Peace! Tranquil, halcyon peace!
Where does she bestow equity?
Lo and behold! She now keeps
Only the interests of inequity.

Simple is her mien, honey-sweet her utterances,
Her figure is draped in a bright white costume.
Beware, O Yudhisthira! For the fangs and tresses
Of this she-cobra are dipped in lethal venom.

She often fills King Jarasandha's (5) dungeons,
Brimful with captive kings and princely miens,
Sometimes she drinks blood, while it swears,
Betimes, the cascading stream of hot tears.

It was not that peace whose pyres
Blazed in the battle of Kuru princes,

It wasn't an ill-portending crusade
That shot from Arjuna's arrowhead.

It was a she-serpent, the devouress of others' interests,
It was that which blazed in the battle of selfish interests;
It was an unrestrainable, unenduring flame of valiance,
That sparked from Parth's arrowhead with radiance.

For, when the Dame of Peace did not even care
To stay, bestowing a few needs that were fair;
The brave Arjuna hurled himself upon her,
Fierce as Death, holding her life on the spur.

Who's a sinner? He that pilfers and wrests
From the other his just 'n' equitous rights?
Or he who in the quest for justice fights,
Toppling the coronets of many martinets?

CANTO - IV

A great pillar of the faith and to celibacy wed,
The majestic bearer of boundless might and main;
A unique ascetic who did ever on the earth tread,
One whom the world found, and yet lost in vain.

He happily forsook the crown to uphold the faith,
And for the love of it, he exhaled his last breath;
Perchance, there was none in the princely fold
As heroic as Bhisma or, indeed, as high-souled;

Sprawled on the sharp, speary arrow-heads like an elephant,
Exhausted, as the worn-out eagle, as the fatigued serpent,
Crushing mortality with the weight of a life bravely spent,
Pressing on death, holding consciousness with firm intent,

Thus lay Bhisma narrating to Kaunteya the tale of battle,
Threading his manifold griefs in the string of remembrance.
And when the heart's agog, ruffled ocean was all a-rattle,
The wise sire gave vent to his anguish with all fervence:

"He who denies justice is the one who triggers the fight,
O Yudhisthira! It is no sin to fight for one's just right.
Hell awaits those who yield to means foul and unfair,
Not those who the wrongs and vices of the battle dare.

"Not for nothing one yearns to fight against the others,
To kill or get oneself killed in the battlefield by others;

Man doesn't ever wish to break even an uneasy peace,
He labours on with love's spirit in so far as it keeps.

"This love of peace restrains only the noble 'n' good,
It fails to impede the onrush of the vile 'n' the wicked;
For the wicked scarcely but ever appreciate the good,
And oft deem humility to be the creed of the coward.

"As time passes on, the plight worsens much further,
The sequence of inequities becomes more severe;
Then, on some fateful day, there is a huge explosive vent,
As noble men *sans* fear hurl themselves on the malevolent.

"But do not consider only the vanquished and the victor,
The battle's twin leaders, as the authors of this terrible stir;
The whole world can't flare up because of a few odd men,
Nor can be moved by the fate of those who're the chosen.

"O Yudhisthira! A mountain of fire doesn't burst up suddenly,
Nor do thunderbolts ever unleash from a sky that's all empty;
Lolling tongues of flame spurt out of the earth's red-hot vent
And awesome flashes of lightning strike the dusty firmament.

"The Mahabharata war wasn't just a clash between two houses,
There lay in it an incendiary heap of numerous personal grouses;
It wasn't just an evil aftermath of the struggle of the Kuru band,
It was a conflagration that engulfed in its blight the whole land.

"Poison winds had since ages been blowing in the firmament,
And the earth mutely bore the forest's all-consuming fire;
One and all were ready to set right their mutual avengement,
Everyone since long was looking for some pretext for war.

"Someone was burning somewhere with envy of someone else's gallantry,
Somewhere someone was seething with anger at someone else's cruelty,
Somewhere the majesty of a king was at the root of the other king's torment,
Someone somewhere nurtured with care vengeance's venomous serpent.

"Radheya [1] yearned to honour his pledge of Parth's slaughter,
Drupada [2] desired to settle scores with Drona, in a manner,
Shakuni [3] longed to pay back the debt of his deceased father
And to bring to dust the Kuru kingdom's high-flying banner.

"It wasn't Shakuni's love of Suyodhana, but his guileful manoeuvring,
To act as his well-wisher, but in sooth to keep his anger simmering.
The rancorous fires, wherever they were, kept on thus smouldering,
As though restive for bursting in the battle-field, forever seething.

"Whosoever were incensed by the promptings of the Lord,
In their wrath had bound themselves into a wilful accord.
The slaughter of Shishupal[4] had not yet subdued their conceit,
With redoubled pride they did in silence fret, ready for deceit.

"Engulfed and divided by mutual jealousy, rancour and quarrel,
People were since long arrayed in belligerent camps for battle,
They rose, with crackling flames in their hearts burning hot,
Their sheaths stuffed with swords, their bow-strings fully taut.

"And if any residual ingredient of vice
In the death-potion was hitherto absent,
O Yudhisthira! The Rajasuya Sacrifice[5]
Accomplished that peremptory intent.

"Even though desire is noble, yet the fruit
Thereof, it is upto Providence to proffer,
The nectar-tree bears lethal poison in its fruit:
Strange, inscrutable are the ways of Nature.

"In crowning you as the land's sovereign king,
Consecrated by Rajasuya's sacrificial offering,
Lord Keshava[6] had pondered over the measure,
Of bringing about oneness, the greatest treasure.

"This, in sooth, served but no other purpose
Than blowing up the world in flames, a-seething,
Despicable envy was sown, and sprouted thus
In the wan hearts of many a vanquished king.

"Nor did they pause ever to heed or to comprehend
The good motive behind Lord Keshava's guileless aim;
Biased, they could apprehend only a malicious intent,
Wary of the growing strength of Indraprastha[(7)] kingdom.

"The string of impediments that serves as an obstacle
In regarding the venerated as indeed the venerable,
Points forward to the egotism hidden inside man,
To the inescapable predicament of human illusion.

"The canopy of the Indraprastha crown
Was the pride of the entire kingdom;
It wouldn't besmirch anyone's renown,
To proffer due obeisance to that diadem.

"But there were many who felt peeved
At this sinless, unblemished salutation,
Their wayward, aberrant minds perceived
It as their pride's impending devastation.

"In the homage they paid to the emperor
They discerned but their own helplessness,
In the progress and prosperity of another
They saw their own eventual subservience.

"The celebration of the great Rajasuya Sacrifice
Seemed to them like a battle stratagem, a vice;
It meant the ruthless pursuit of a selfish thing,
On the part of a clever and self-seeking king.

"O Dharmaraja! None does really desire,
To part with one's vanity and pride,

Or to bow gladly before a lofty power,
With all his wilful sense in stride.

"All of them who came under your banner
Didn't come because of your love 'n' honour;
Some came because they held you in high gear,
While others came because of your sword's fear.

"Whatsoever were their personal feelings, for sure
One thing lay rooted in everyone's mental cogitation:
That their sparkling crowns would scarce be secure,
Their honour could not command revered salutation.

"In their doubting minds lurked fears random,
Of their servility and subsequent thralldom,
To them it seemed as if an imperial hegemony
Would emerge from the Rajasuya ceremony.

"The Sacrifice did, in sooth, suppress
The dignity of many kings 'n' princes,
Of many wielders of power and affluence
Of great heroes and still greater veterans.
"It's true that you had welcomed with alacrity
The monarchs, princes, and gathered nobility,
Persuading them all with prayer and parity,
With sweet and pretty words, with humility.

"But such vain entreaties can scarce recompense
The price of the rare gem of freedom, so scarce;
For the ever-blazing, erupting pangs of anguish
That wrack the mind's regions, cannot diminish.

"Only an indolent prince, a moronic dud,
Can feel gratified at the placating word,
And at the conqueror's apparent civility,
Or at the endearing hug of the adversary.

"A wise king soothes his enemy's fright
By holding him close in his warm clasp;
But never lets his discerning heart alight
In his opponent's wide outstretched grasp.

"The ill-will of kings 'n' princes were not thus quenched
By their protestations of respect for the sacrificial offering,
As they returned from Indraprastha, with envy drenched,
Each one was laden with the thought of a different bearing.

"O Dharmaraja! Don't you indeed remember
The doom-portending words of sage Vyas,
That awe-inspiring prophecy of the future
That he uttered at the end of the Sacrifice:

"A congregation of stars, in an evil constellation,
Has been of late conjoining in the high heavens,
The world shall, forsooth, break into smithereens
By an impending, all-annihilating conflagration.

"Somehow for thirteen years alone,
In the land peace will prevail upon,
Then a deafening bloom will blow,
And soon a mighty war will follow.

"The destruction shall be dreadful, and amid the din
Death shall dance and dally around with devastation,
Upon the earth shall prevail a reign of frightful ruin,
And high above shall rise the cries of lamentation.

"These were the words of the wise seer,
They were not wild conjectures of fear;
Vyas knew the world was led to predicament
Each and every eerie and evanescent moment.

"All were contented by the sacrificial offering,
But the saint's heart was restless and quivering,

He alone was aware of the devilish fire
Billowing from the flames of the altar.

"In the midst of the whole assembly
He had bidden everyone to be wary,
At each step he urged them earnestly,
To observe restraint was his homily.

"But does the vain man, with passion burning,
Ever restrain himself or curb his yearning?
Does he take fright now at the direful sorrow,
That's well on its way to occur on the morrow?

"No sooner was the year gone
Than Death blew forth its horn,
Of a sudden the clouds of misfortune converged
On Indraprastha, and calamity its head upsurged.

"None knew that calamity
Will spread itself in a trice,
That a curse on the country
Will emanate from the dice.

"None knew that Suyodhana's steadfastness
Will leave him in such a hurrying haste,
That from the pit of the sacrificial furnace,
A ruinous and ravaging flame will burst.

"Even so, it's true, O Dharmaraja!
That its bilious blaze was age-old;
It lay simmering for quite an age
In Suyodhana's bosom's inmost fold.

"On the day when the bird's eye in the target
Was shot in the arena by Arjuna's arrowhead,
The evil flame of malice secretly did a vent find
From the concealed corners of Suyodhana's mind.

"It was this that finally led to the dynasty's doom,
The all-consuming flames of the shellac-house,
The fraud played by Shakuni in the gambling room,
The banishment of Pandavas, their fret 'n' grouse.

"It wasn't, in sooth, Draupadi's modesty
That was outraged in the royal assembly,
It was this very fire of fearsome ferocity
That crackled and blazed up dauntlessly.

"As the raiment of the helpless princess,
Brazenly was tugged, stripped, undraped,
So did, hitherto unveiled, this vile blaze,
Lay its guise bare and gleefully played.

"In the extracting web of her sinuous hair
Swayed the strands of this sinister flare,
In the piled heaps of her disrobed attire,
Evil's disguised face was exposed bare.

"Yet in this sordid, saddening state
She was saved by her spiritual fate,
Her long-flowing, unending raiment
Shone like a robe dazzling luminescent.

"But the hellish fire of Suyodhana's rancour
Yet did shamelessly dance, naked and bare,
As though testing the limit of his effrontery
And the virility and manhood of this country.

"But alas! I cannot say why on that day
Both, you 'n' I, lost in the honour's fray?
Why did not the rush of blood's thrust,
Erupt through the virile veins and burst?

"The banner of man's repute and dignity
Lay despoiled 'n' uprooted in the country,
The day a woman, by men helpless wrought,
Shrieked cries of anguish and invoked God.

"This awesome, apocalyptic war ought to have
Commenced on that evil, sinister, devilish day,
This mire and slush of disgrace ought to have
By the sword been blood-washed that very day.

"They dragged from inside the royal household
The shy, inculpable, and half-clad family bride,
Brought her in thrall before the assembled fold,
Having won her in the game of dice, as she cried.

"Amid everyone they continued *sans* fear
To strip her of the costume she did wear,
Yet the dumbfounded gallants of the court
Against this didn't utter a word of support.

"Who would strive to contemplate or comprehend
This practice of a New Order, so unique 'n' strange?
The yet-unbegotten posterity would sure reprehend
And spit upon us, as well upon their tainted heritage.

"Yet my spirit begins to instantly burn,
Stirring that event in the memory's urn,
As though inside me a knife
Rips through the heart's hive.

"Fie! Fie! Everlasting humiliation on me,
The royal bride was disrobed before me,
Before my shameless eyes, the modesty
Of Draupadi was outraged by perfidy.

"And how I've lived on? Nor was the earth
Shaken up, or quaked upon its axial fulcrum,
Nor did the vault of heaven open up in wrath,
Nor thunderbolts crashed on my olden frame.

"Like as a flaming ball of fire
I have lived my life's long span,
It was not blood, but liquid fire,
Running ceaselessly in my vein.

"This was a proud man who could brook
Not the unseeming arrogance of any crook,
Who could not stay quiet or speechless ever,
At wrongs and inequities against whosoever.

"Thus I'm besmirched with undeserved blemish
That cannot be wiped off by external cleansing,
By writhing within one's inner self with anguish,
Or by crying hoarse with repentant weeping.

"I'll depart soon, though with a lurking sense
Of suspicion over my manhood's true essence,
Yet, O Dharmaraja! Mark my words carefully,
Since I'll be gone, I bestow unto you this homily:

"The creed of heroic bravery lies on the path
Of treading on the ever burning sheets of blaze;
The creed of chivalrous bravery lies on the path
Of dancing intrepidly on the sharp sword's edge.

"The creed of valiance lies on the path
Of bearing arrows on the breast bravely,
The creed of valiance lies on the path
Of drinking the lethal potion gleefully.

"The creed of true heroism lies in lighting up
A bright flame on the palms, staying unfurled,

In offering the head as libation, in holding up
A non-pareil lesson of sacrifice to the world.

"Above all, the best human creed, and its source,
Lies in being ever and more radiant with a glow,
In possessing an irrepressible vigour and force,
In bearing not ever, even a soft touch of the foe.

"The bravest of the heroes relinquish the force
Of reason and tread blindfold on their course;
Readily do they all ascend the sacrificial altar,
Offering themselves to flames, never to falter.

"The moment a man's valour goes to seek
The counsel of reason, it becomes meek,
Perforce, it has to gulp the cup of shame,
And shed bravery's self-radiating flame.

"In sooth, the pitcher of reason is laden
With sweet soft water, with cool nectar,
But never forget that in times ill-begotten,
The ambrosia is turned into lethal water.

"Wary reason does not ponder over
The cognizance of shame or honour,
She thinks much; she keeps doused
The flame of valour that has aroused.

"True, it was reason that had doused
The glowing embers of thy manhood,
And closed your eyes at the tragedy
Of the brazen disrobing of Draupadi.

"True, it was reason that had bound
My sense to doubt's cowardly hound,
And the moment had long passed whence
I could arouse my natural conscience.

"Youth always struts and frets with pride,
With head held high and bow in readiness,
But old age, frail and infirm, lags in stride,
Is weighed down under reason's stress.

"On gazing at the upsurge of youth
It sinks in mournful melancholy;
The scared reason holds its breath,
Standing aside in wait respectfully.

"Lest it be swept away, reason is afraid,
Like a straw in a whirling sweeping tide,
The thought of flood excites its dread,
And skulkingly it does in its cellar hide.

"Behind the bloom of youth lies a sequence
Of an unceasing and arduous perseverance,
For the world is ever filled with fresh light,
Fresh fragrance, fresh smell and fresh sight.

"But the cunning reason forever lies in wait
For its prey, does the coming moment await,
When the tide of youth would slowly weary
With age, making it easy to devour its quarry.

"For, in sooth, whenever the warm thrust
Of young blood mellows down, even just,
Whenever the stream of life in full measure
Ceases somewhere for a moment of leisure.

"Soon reason, the wily huntress, springs her net
And man falls a prey to her magic enchantment;
Life proffers yet more troubles for men to fret,
With new worries and many a new entanglement.

"Forgiveness or revenge, which of the twain
Behoves the dignity of the common humanity?
Submission or revolt, which of the twain
Is the remedy for an injudicious malady?

"Which is better, strength or reason?
Is the sword best, or is it persuasion?
Which is better, the blood-besmirched feat,
Or the dire, dismal, death-bringing defeat?

"Which of the twin flames is truly pristine?
Is it that of the heart, or of the soul divine?
Is the good sense of a lustre-dimmed age
Better, or better is the gift of young age?

"It's a terrible weariness of our life -
That which we call the life's autumn;
The old and aging veterans do strive
For ideals, bearing arrows of sarcasm.

"Under the spell of reason does old age
Spin helplessly upon the wheel of Karma(8),
It's not as quick of doubt as of courage,
Not quick to respond to Time 'n' Dharma(9).
"But Time, the devourer, by then flees away,
Stealing the valour of the valiants of the day,
And, soon, the age-stupefied man lies indeed
Deep in the mire of many a remorseful deed.

"So did I dwell in the kingdom of Suyodhana
Reaping wryly the blighted harvest of old age;
My heroic valour did fume and fret in vain,
Lying cribbed 'n' confined in the bodily cage.

"Neither did I do the welfare of the Kauravas
Nor did I render good to the brave Pandavas,

The autumn of life preyed upon my judgment,
Placing my conscience in dubious predicament.

"Both love 'n' faith were dear to my duty
It was indeed quite a ticklish verdict.
Hence, to the one I bestowed my body,
While to the other I gave my spirit.

"But as the sullen, sombre clouds cleared,
The radiant light of a sweet life appeared
And, of a sudden, in these desolate sands,
A stream of love poured on Bharat's lands.

"In this way the call of duty withered,
As the victory of love was declared,
My body 'n' limbs were given as gifts galore
To those who had claimed my heart before.

"Bhisma fell because of the weight of his years,
He was not felled by the prickly arrows of Parth;
Piercing the mists of age, it was verily my youth
That had re-emerged from across Time's barriers.

"Unto love did I my spirit yield,
To action I got my arms dedicated,
Thus in the Kurukshetra battlefield
I came with my heart contented.

"I thought my dilemma would itself remove
By conceding to this fair, rightful bifurcation,
But I didn't know that love's bond and groove,
Were much more knotty than that of action.

"Holding up high the faith's spectre,
Action did arduously take my service,
Yet in quietude it made me a gesture,
Prompting my feelings to do sacrifice.

"O Dharmaraja! In the crucial hour,
The spurious veil is oft uncovered;
And man's true character and power
Lie before the entire world unbared.

"The hazy story unfolded clearly forth,
As the fierce battle raged yet ferociously,
And the long-suppressed spirit of youth,
Did rise up to bestow my love graciously.

"The illusory spell of reason was broken
And the false veil of action was taken
Away from my body, my soul, and my eyes,
As the voice of love yelled its rapturous cries:

"Come hither Parth! Take your due, of course,
Come hither! Strike me dead without remorse;
Unbearable now are the pangs of separation,
Come ye bowman! Reach me to Love's haven.

"The stream of love that was obstructed
On the day of the celibatarian pledge,
After long has on Kurukshetra erupted
And engulfed me in its swirling maze.

"Never before I had heard pleasant breezes sing,
Nor did the bower of my desires shake or swing;
Never ever I'd heard birds' notes, so mellifluous,
Rising from the cluster of leaves, so melodious.

"Never before I'd offered a bunch of flowers
To anyone; nor did I ever indulge and endear
The wishes of someone, nor did even once
Bestow myself in gift to someone very dear.

"The feeling of unfulfilment 'n' its murmur,
Lay concealed in my heart's secret corner,
While life slipped away too surreptitiously
To hide itself in the hollow of a tree shyly.

"That same feeling led me into the midst of battle,
Encouraging me to climb the altar of high ideal;
That same feeling of unfulfilment now speaks
In agony, through wounds and injuries it drips.

"In sooth, I was most careful and much wary,
Having tied my life with the bond of restraint
And my bow was strung up, aimed and ready,
To shoot the marks of any tender sentiment.

"But I wasn't aware yet that an enchantress,
Trod over the internal spheres of my senses,
That in this abysmal pit's dark recesses,
A luminous flame of feeling was ablaze.

"I came hither to fight this sanguinary war
As Suyodhana's grand army's commander,
I came not on the Kurukshetra battle-field
To die for love, but to wrest victory's shield.
"Verily, my faith lay entrenched
In the invincible bow of Parth,
And its frightful arch ever filled
My heart with a gleeful mirth.

"It's true, I wished the well-being of Pandavas
From the real and profound depths of my heart,
But my body had been sold before to Kauravas,
To the Kuru throne, to pay for the worth of salt.

"Even so has love her riches won,
Having pierced the array of my duty;
It's now proven, one who has won
The heart must also receive the body.

"Had the immortality of sweet love dawned
Early upon my consciousness and desire,
The fate of the land would not be pawned,
To the wounds of the Kurukshetra war.

"O Dharmaraja! By treating with disdain
Many a soft, sweet and emotional strain,
Methinks I too have pushed and hurled,
Into the inferno of battle, this whole world.

"At the onset of my life's dreary span,
I took up the tough vow of celibacy,
And sought ever and always to ban
All soft feelings and heart's delicacy.

"For I didn't believe that the mission of love
Was superior to that of action's greater hub,
That the ever-blazing flame of tenderness
Was mightier than the call of duteousness.

"A bow in my hand, a quiver upon my back,
The knowledge of social ethics lay in my heart,
Of nothing else beside did I ever follow track
Ever in the tedious course of my life's chart.

"Whenever did some tender feelings enliven,
In the arcane recesses of my inward heaven,
They had soon to bow down to the rules
Of my courtly duties and my principles.

"Thus was my heart wrecked and riven,
By Suyodhana's deed, so flagrantly driven,
But I could do naught, being bound by duty,
And my principles proved a brighter entity.

"Assigning even the right of discipline,
Voluntarily into the hands of principle,
I became a slave, being ever dependent,
Upon the clemencies of my temperament.

"Reason was life's empress, so kind,
While the heart was a mere subject,
Scared to truly lay bare its mind,
With clarity of beliefs on the subject.

"It could not tell me loud 'n' clear that I'm amiss:
'O Bhisma! Whither are you going aimlessly?
You have become the bearer of the staff of justice,
Why do you keep enduring inequity endlessly?'

"My heart's love I showered on the Pandavas,
While with my body I served the Kauravas,
But what good could be verily accomplished
By such perseverance, dimmed 'n' diminished?

"The fierce and ever-expanding animosity
Of Suyodhana against the Pandava fraternity,
Within me was reflected as the inimicality
Between an eager heart and a serving body.

"But ever did wary reason delude me,
Never did it let me venture out free,
Nor it let me claim my right, ever,
To bestow it upon my heart's altar.

"Oft and ever it laid bare some dreams
Of the self-pacification of the rancour,
It counselled me even to forget, at times,
Who was a friend and who was a stranger.

"At other times it said to me loud, 'Your advance
Soon would cause others to run out of patience,
There'll be insurrection everywhere and the channel
Of law and order will explode surely *sans* trammel.

"It oft prevented me from entering the woods,
By stirring the dormant flames of valorous fires;
It oft deprived me in varied ways of the fruits,
The realization of which were my heart's desires.

" I'm led to think now of what would have happened,
Had I never listened to cold reason's fecund advice,
Had I but known it no sooner than it had happened,
That the sacred visage of justice was to be its price.

"Would it were that I could ever cleanse
The sin of politics in love's potion,
Would it were that I could ever coalesce
The tenets of punishment with compassion.

"A tale that the tongue failed to iterate
To authority's callous and stony breast,
Would it were that I could resuscitate
It with the pen of regret and reiterate,

"Would it were that I could perforce liberate
My pulsating heart from the sway of my head,
That I could ever come down from the high stand
Of power and give the persecuted a helping hand;

"Would it were that I could raise without any fear
The banner of sedition and spread it everywhere,
That I could dare and challenge the malevolence
Of Suyodhana, being on the side of righteousness.

"Perchance, Suyodhana would have been struck with fear,
At each step, then, he would have taken care not to smear;

Perchance, thus, the land of Bharat wouldn't have fallen
Into the cauldron of this all-annihilating conflagration.

"But when all is thought, said and done
There's nothing new of which to speak,
Forget the tale and forgive the bygone,
Let the world move in a maiden epoch.

"Peace be unto my soul: I got every fraction
Of the fruits of action before my last journey,
The buttress of both love and conviction
Were at once and easily accessible to me."

CANTO - V

O Sharade![1] I'm a man of this epoch in transition's torpid phase
I'm the ever-lingering Dwapar[2] standing on top of the Kali[3] age;
It was in the quest of a shade for a world in affliction's direful maze
That I had come, with hope, this far in the annals of history's page.

But, ah! Here, too, the whole firmament is set ablaze,
And the wind is blowing in gusts of incendiary rage;
From eternity's chasm emanates a tumultuous boom,
And from the angry sea the din of the dance of doom.

Here lies heavy the crackling sound of wood 'n' forest burning;
Here a dreadful and blazing volcano of fire is forever bursting;
Is it the smell of decaying flesh from these pages wafting?
Who's in flames? Whose horrid smoke is hereof emerging?

Here the breast of the scared earth is with iron-bars impaled;
Whose blood-besmirched banner of conquest is here spread?
Who's it that dances here wielding the sword of demolishment?
His body with blood bestrewn, his tongue lolling like a serpent.

Is it just a horse that's running, or is it a man's prideful passion?
Is it a Sacrifice that's being performed, or is it world's destruction?
That which the poniard cuts through and accumulates with ease,
Is it just a pool of water, or is it the blood of the human species?

The libations that the regal princes carry helplessly as a duty,
Are these gifts for the Sacrifice, or the pearls of their dignity?

Is it just the fuel encrusted oblation that does on the altar blaze?
Or is it the scotched pride of an usurped king that's on rampage?

Do the priests recite the *Vedas*[4] or the hymns of conflagration?
Do they quench the flames of life, or enkindle life's aspiration?
Is this grey smoke a measure of the victor's glorious reputation?
Or, is it the fuming and fretting of a king's helpless indignation?

Is it the chant of benediction, or a blazing incandescence?
Is it the sacrificial ablution, or a plunging in bloodshed?
The bright red mark that adorns the emperor's forehead,
Is it sandal-paste, or a ruddy mark of someone's vengeance?

And as the sword dazzles, the poet's pen too moves ahead,
Composing copious paeans of passion, fire, and arrowhead.
O Sharade! No sooner spite returned victorious from the battle
Than hastily a hostess emerged to cheer it up from your castle.

She came with a platter of welcome in her dainty hands,
Chanting couplets of applause in her mellifluous voice;
She lit the ceremonial lamp; she did sing and rejoice,
To shower on the deity of destruction her gaudy garlands.

With her raiment's end she rubs out the blood and the ordure,
Variously she adorns its form with many a beauteous feature;
Decorating its image she wore it in her breath, and hence
Immortalized it as heroism in her sweet, melodious strains.

Malice, having lost in the battle-field was thus laid waste,
While the flames of justice, being victorious, became sacred.
It's true that if appearance can be transformed by conquest,
So can the heinous sin of murder be wiped from the forehead.

Being so, who can ever weigh jubilation with remorse?
Who can probe his heart, having closed his eyes 'n' ears?
Or think that if the slaughter of a man is a misdeed,

How is the slaughter of so many not an evil deed?

Of none he is ever afraid, in the absence of battle,
Why not fearlessly he kills men indiscriminately;
All the limits he exceeds in the gory field of battle.
Whence he gets the right to slay humans wantonly?

But a wise man stands quietly in history's page,
His eyes with tears filled, for profusely he'd cried.
In his heart is lit pity's sweet and gentle blaze,
Trampled under his feet lies his blood-red pride.

The dame of victory stands before with a laurel,
Anxiously she awaits him in her bashful grace;
But Dharmaraja fails to discern this fair damsel,
Scarce does he remember this maiden's face.

Kaunteya stands up there, but only with his body,
While his mind roams in the domain of Beauty,
The domain where spite melts away completely,
Where the hardened steel is tempered absolutely.

Where man wanders shorn of the tie of attachment,
Where a human being is not frightened of his kin,
Where there is a reign of peace and no despairment,
Where the feeling of selfishness is forsaken as a sin,

Where the minds of men are ruled by pity's fair-faced cherubim,
Where love controls all, where justice is a matter of free giving,
Where it's better to drink one's tears than other's blood-stream,
Where one may renounce the crown forever and beg for a living.

A realm where the warmth of gore cannot go,
Where the scalps of men are not cursed by war,
Where life is nourished under equality's shadow,
Where in each house is lit the lamp of nectar.

O the dame of victory! With blood is soiled thy dress,
Your visage is no different form Death's devilish face,
Your livery is aflame with a frill of fiery flare,
A mist of doom is filled in your swarthy hair.

O the all-devouring serpent of Kurukshetra war!
Wipe off the redness of blood from thy mien,
He's in quest of a fruit steeped full with nectar,
Whom thou art restless for choosing as companion.

Behold him there high in the fathomless firmament,
Where he soars away in pursuit of his intendment,
To fetch for the mother earth a stream of nectar,
A river of equality, a giver of love's sweet water.

Peace will arise from the sequence of such dreams,
And the world will be liberated from Death's whims;
Thus will remorse be victorious in the victor's heart,
When his eyes will, with pity's clouds, be overcast.

The day the victor will weep on manslaughter for what it is,
The day he will, with tears, his crimson gore and filth cleanse,
The path of human triumph will open that very great moment,
As the frightened earth's fortune will proclaim loud its advent.

O Doom's daughter! O victory's inebriated damsel!
Beside whom do you stand with your nuptial laurel?
The wielder of the sword has long past bidden adieu,
This's a man who'll squander his empire and its residue.

You can't ever get him in this blood-bestrewn guise,
You can't awaken this ascetic with arrows of arrogance;
Your hands will not be tied in his hands as a prize,
Behind lies your home; this is an abode of penance.

Until this dweller-in-the-sky returns from his habitation,
Until this mendicant renounces the altar of abnegation;

Till then your passion-bred hues wouldn't flourish,
Till then the flowers of your garland would perish.

However much reason might solace heart's lamentation,
Nature doesn't easily relinquish her right of retaliation.

Bereft of any means the human heart may cease,
But the ruthless onrush of anguish cannot ease.

For how can artifice ever conceal from our vigilant eyes
The desolate and devastated stretch which before us lies.

Thus ceaselessly flows the unending tale from Pitamaha's lips,
And as Kaunteya hears it, he's overcome with grief and weeps.

"Yes, Pitamaha: all is done, acted; nothing else does remain,
What remains in our sight is nothing but Death's domain:

"Where the mighty, awesome, terrible spectre of Death lies buried,
Sombre, still as a gigantic corpse, as if it were worn out and wearied.

"Bearing mangled bodies in the fold of her apparel, stained with bleeding,
The dejected earth, mother of dead sons, lies dumb in doleful brooding.

"The heart seems to choke from this rottening, putrid fetid,
As the wind holds its breath and flees off with hurried speed.

"The despondent, frigid day-star sheds its warmth hesitatingly,
And the moon scuds through the clouds to hide its face silently.

"These guests of Death, flocks of forest-cats and jackals,
Dogs, vultures and crows, devour the scattered victuals.

"Manu's[(5)] sons become the feed of animals; ah! Is't man's end?
Ah! The heroes of Bharat's land have met with such sordid end.

"Their mighty arms, which dangled on both sides of their bodies once,
That oft became the beloved's necklace, and at times the enemy's curse.

"The robust and resplendent eagle's wings, once invincible and great,
Now are fearlessly ripped off by the wolves and dogs of the forest.

"The human scalp which the crows tear up with their beaks,
Perchance, was the repository once of progressive streaks.

"The human breast which the horrendous vultures split off and eat,
Perchance, contained once a good poet's love-filled, sobre spirit.

"The catastrophe hasn't only the human numbers dismembered,
In its wake, it has many a prized and rare crown plundered.
"The best of men, brave and dauntless, the bright paragons of valiance,
The incarnate foundations of the faith, of wisdom, of art and science—

"One and all were slain in the battle; the poor earth, lacking lustre
And bereft of her gems, lost all that she possessed in Kurukshetra.

"Prosperity, splendour and beauty - all these vanished with Duryodhana,
What remains in my cursed sinful hands is but a dry and bare skeleton.

"This skeleton is memory's curse for the dead's vanity,
It is but a torment for the hearts of the living humanity.

"This bare skeleton is but a token of Yudhisthira's victory,
It is but the ignominious gift of Mahabharata's history.

"A land whereupon the wounded moan in utter distress,
Where a sky, filled with screams of pity, reverberates.

"A continent where unto the dust goes the remains of success,
A blighted land where flowers of prosperity are burnt to ashes.

"These remainders of Doom: this land, cursed and death-desiring:

This was the boon that could come in the bower of my well-being.

"They are all gone, the heroes, long ago in Suyodhana's train,
What remains behind is this ruined land, strewn with corpses;
The bewailing of mothers for their dead sons, too, does remain,
What remains at last is the mournful guise of young widows;
Peace and happiness, delight and passion, have all vanished,
While poverty, pathos, and misery are left in hapless entirety;
In the hands of Fate what does remain for the unvanquished?
What remains is the remnant of a ruined 'n' wrecked prosperity.

"The battle is quenched; but ah! Still the agonized earth,
Downcast and dismayed, is frightened to her very breath;
On the faces of men and women the grim, grisly spectre
Of the all-annihilating Doom lies still as the sole victor;
Both the earth and the welkin are sombre and dejected,
And a heavy pall of gloom is in every direction spread;
None knows whether the mother earth, scared 'n' afraid,
Is yet imbued with life or, like her many sons, is dead.

"O Pitamaha! Behold awhile this forlorn crematory,
See! How they descend, the ghosts of bygone glory;
Adorning the prince of Kurus in a variety of ways,
They sing rapturously the lofty paeans of his praise;
See! How they ridicule me in their sullen whispers,
Gesturing out to me the cut off and torn cadavers;
Harken now their rumbling, roaring peals of scorn,
As they slight and sully me with derisive disdain.

"They say: 'O Yudhisthira! Oftentimes you did express
Great and noble ideas of human virtue and goodness;
To one and all did you dispense many a wise sermon
Of penance, renunciation, mercy, and compassion;
More often thou were ready to share in equal measure
The sordid suffering of others with thy own displeasure;
For the sake of justice you gave up home 'n' wealth,

And dwelt deep inside the forest to uphold the faith.

"Was it all true, or was it all nothing but a clever exhibition?
The wily renunciation of one without courage of conviction;
One whose very deeds roused in the people remorse,
Who formed thus, by pity, his own formidable force;
Was it, in sooth, tolerance; or was it but the flame
Of vengeance that burnt secretly inside your breast?
Was it only principle, or was it a glaring stratagem,
To cover in vain the dubious face of your self-interest?

"No sooner the pulse of the populace came in your hand
Than the gallants and the heroes gathered to your band;
It was then that you abandoned the guise of pity in utter haste,
As the thought of wreaking vengeance tormented your breast;
It was then that the Pandavas revealed their true appearance,
Having cast off the sham jewels of renunciation and penance;
It was then that calamity loomed large in the welkin,
And the clouds of war began to thunder in a loud din.

"Say O Yudhisthira! Did you not ever fume and fret
At your suffering, and at Suyodhana's self-indulgence?
Say honestly, did your breath not ever burn or grate,
On beholding the Kuru prince's power and affluence?
But the Pandavas shrouded their spite with penance,
Thus they deceived the whole world by posing saintly,
Although their hearts blazed with flames of vengeance,
They lamented, rued and repented their fates apparently.

"When this all-consuming spite burst into an incendiary conflict,
There was no sin you didn't commit, no wrongs you didn't inflict;
You uttered a lie for committing your preceptor's assassination;
Because of you Drona was decapitated, while sitting in meditation;
At long last, at whose behest, you invented a new rule of fighting,
When Bhima battered and broke the thighs of the Kuru warrior,
And at whose behest he severed the breast of the dying princeling,

Swallowing up the gushing stream of blood with vengeful savour.

"Why don't you now enclose her in your warm embrace,
For the sake of whom did you these gory sins commit?
Why are you not afraid anymore of Draupadi's sullen face,
Why don't you now kick away victory with your feet?
Why don't you accept, and partake of the pleasures
Of splendour 'n' prosperity of Kuru's ample treasures?
Say, O Yudhisthira! The victor of the battle of Kurukshetra
Why don't you now sit on the throne and hold the spectre?

"There are no more obstacles. The Pandavas may decorate
And adorn their victorious heads with the royal coronet.
Relieved of the grim threat from Suyodhana and his band
They can raise their heads happily and stride free the land;
They can acquire now whatsoever riches they may desire,
And fill their abodes with affluence, and for more aspire;
No more gallant warriors or heroes are left to oppose,
They can now reign gleefully over the wailing widows.

"O Pitamaha! Indeed it's all true: that the planet
Earth, the bride of heroes, weeps like a dowager;
Look! She crushes with her forehead her bracelet,
Effacing thus the symbolic mark of her coverture;
Lo and behold her! The merciless damsel of victory,
How mad has become, how drunken and diabolical;
Look! That now she prepares for her nuptial spree,
At the place where the poor earth is laid for funeral.

"How'll I ever raise up from her knees and embrace
In my arms this mournful and bewailing doweress?
How'll I ever enclose in my lap the widowed spouse,
The funeral pyres of whose husband yet didn't douse?
Lest what's left of my renown should turn to dust
I shall no more display for riches any intent or lust.

Indeed, I'm slurred with the ignominy of causing war,
But hence I shall no more further besplurge this scar.

"O Sire! Were it known to me that property
It is which is the ultimate end of all enmity,
Had I been aware of this hidden demon, so fiery,
In the dismal days of my forest retreat, so dreary,
If it were known, then, what to talk of Draupadi?
I wouldn't have paid heed even to Krishna's gospel,
O Pitamaha! Were it known to me in the early spell,
I would not have taken to arms and brought this hell.

"But alas! It was a dark night darkened further by illusion,
The radiant morrow of today was nowhere on the horizon;
A mist of confusion spread fully over the benighted zone,
The beauteous light of knowledge hadn't till then shone;
The battle wasn't barely an outcome of my blind anger,
For I too was spurred and incited by the lure of lucre,
Ah! Pitamaha, I didn't know yet the most revealing
Of all truths, and one that was the most frightening.

"Nothing stirred my heart, as the hordes marched ahead,
No thoughts ever came up to ask me whither I was led,
Wherefore, and to settle what old score with motherland,
Did I proceed to invite calamity's blast on the battle-land?
What it is whence I derived my inspiration and flare?
Is it the Kuru treasure, or is it Draupadi's locks of hair?
Wherefore do I drive on: is it to rub off my disgrace?
Or is it for the thirst of pleasure that I stride apace?

"The obliteration of disgrace was nothing but a false pretence;
In sooth, all of us five brothers yearned to seek self-indulgence;
For we too would build a shining and stupendous assembly-hall,
Wherein we would ridicule the Kuru prince, arousing his gall;
Indeed a man does ever wish to conceal his covetousness,
Beneath the sparkle, razzle, and dazzle of his haughtiness;

He fights with all the others because of his own greed,
And makes vain pretensions of many a vengeful deed.
"Our goal of vengeance is now accomplished,
What more fulfillment could have we wished?
We shall no more be angry with or ever strive
Against the three Kuru warriors who're yet alive.
Yet no misdeed it was for us to have pounced
Upon the foe after the battle was announced;
But wouldn't this cornucopia of the Kuru booty
Drown us in sin and make us all the more guilty?

"All would say, Yudhisthira kept the vow of rectitude
Because of his own arrogant and vainglorious attitude;
As the telling hardships of austerity and sacrifice
Began to prey on him, he plunged himself in vice;
He became inane 'n' thoughtless, swarmed by a host
Of worthless pleasures bestowed by the holocaust;
Having failed in keeping his pledge of compassion,
He was consigned to the hell's nethermost dungeon.

"O Pitamaha! Now weigh this all-annihilating battle
Against the hurts and mortifications of a few people;
Say, which of these sins is of a more lethal kind?
Pray, unbare the mysteries of thy brooding mind.
O Sire! But don't stray from your truthful manner,
Or melt with mercy at this poor, unfortunate ruler;
Say, who was accountable for the ruin of everyman,
Was it Suyodhana's tribe or was it Yudhisthira's clan?

"Was it that I should have gone back on my word
Having seen Suyodhana intransigent and firm?
Was it that I should have fallen in the same mud
Wherein he did already wallow and squirm?
Was it that I, too, should have drawn out my sabre
No sooner than I saw him raise his awesome weapon?

Was it that I should have avenged Draupadi's honour
By wreaking ruin and havoc on the whole dominion?

Should the four corners of the earth be doomed to perish
Because someone ran rough-shod over another's blemish?
Should the mother earth be sent to the gallows
Because someone was pierced with fiery arrows?
Should the pride of everyman simmer and blaze
Because the vanity of someone seethed with rage?
Men have swooped on men, become animal fodder,
As the clarion of war sounded the breach of order.

"So don't call it the splendour of main,
For it's poison: this frenzy of contention;
It's the evil flame of bestiality in men,
It's the brimful fury of human passion;
It's the dereliction of reason in man,
For he can't see truth in illusion's mire;
And as the fires burn in the Kuru clan,
Others do find their own homes on fire.

"Why doesn't the world forsake the twain
Who fight with each other, proud and vain?
Mankind should let the twosome to ruin and debris,
Leave them to themselves, as for ruin they both agree;
Strange that man, a receptacle of compassionate vision,
Can shed his blood in a war without rhyme or reason,
But, alas! That he can scarce become neutral
And dare to douse the blazing flames of battle.

"Thus the war of Kurukshetra has come to an end,
Seven of us and three of Kauravas have remained;
But save for some who're fallen, maimed, wounded,
Save for some rendered lame, all others are dead;
None did attain anything, instead they lost all,

Only a few ruined men could survive the toll;
That's all! Only the Pandavas survived the calamity
Having seized thus the throne of the Kuru dynasty.
"I know that it was Kuru throne's power
That lay at the root of this hellish war,
I can now behold the serpent of rapacity,
Unfurled from the tresses of Draupadi,
I now realize it was with avarice did I vie,
It was greed that dimmed the light of my eye;
If this infirmity survived, then how am I a victor?
Here and now one more battle I shall offer.

"This will be a war against the fires of passion,
Whence Yudhisthira will come out with jubilation,
Whence upon the war-shattered vines of humanity
The radiant nectar-fruits of peace will grow aplenty;
Kurukshetra's debris will not be the end of the story,
Men will continue to go farther, to yet higher glory;
Hereafter this son of Manu will no more grumble,
For the lamp of a new faith will thence enkindle.

CANTO - VI

The bright lamp of faith, the candle of divine grace,
When shall, O Lord! Ye enlighten the human race?
Imbued with soft and serene light, and forever to glisten,
When, O Lord! The scorched earth with new sap enliven?

Boundless rains, nectar laden, did on earth descend,
Yet calm and quietude do never on the land unbend.
Forsooth, materialist hedonism flares up *sans* refrain,
Laying jejune the selfless motives of human brain.

Bhisma, Yudhisthira, or the Great Almighty Lord,
Buddha, Ashok, Gandhi, or Jesus, the son of God,
Only in words, in words alone, man commends,
Holds them sublime, his head in reverence bends;
Yet, treading the self-same path so oft-traversed,
Vexing others, and, in turn, himself getting vexed.

Same old abductions, extortions, and vile abasements,
Man's quest of ascent, that treads on others' fragments;
Failing by modest conduct to placate the mutual rage,
Oft the brandishing sword of passion does he raise;
The same chimera of malicious love does he chase,
His life breath, yet underlain in the vile viper's cage.

Life today is helpless no more, as it used to be of yore.
Far ahead has the time rolled; lo! Dwapar is no more,

This world of science, resplendent with splendour and fully equipped,
Sovereign, unfathomed vistas of the inscrutable world have unzipped.
Holding intellect's rudder in hand, rending asunder the bosom of night,
The world in the new land has arrived, bright with luminescent light.

Bizarre and novel is the world that has come to date,
Seated aloft Nature, ever victorious is mankind of late.
Water, power and vapour are all held captives in the hands of Man,
The ascent 'n' descent of air's warmth is slave to the will of Man.
No more, nowhere, any impediments exist,
Streams, hills, rivers, alike, Man can resist.

Bearing atop their heads man's many wishes to pander,
Services galore the Nature's motley elements do render.
Man's commands even the great Varunesh[(1)] does obey,
And the vault of heaven does carry his messages all day.

Space and Time, each ephemeral moment on the brink,
In the formidable fist of the New Age Man does shrink.

Boundless is Man's progress, his ascent a nonpareil feat,
The firmament is in his hands and the world is at his feet.

But to what avail is the progression of human mind,
The heart's dear land has far away been left behind;
Novel feats of brain and brawn Man does ever perform,
As the angelic spirits, in awe 'n' grief, do louder scream.
Not bare knowledge merely do the angels ever desire,
Few balefuls of love 'n' sacrifice do they ever aspire.
Delicate emotions, such as wax, malleable and soft,
Which, as heated, melts in the soul betimes and oft;
Some tender 'n' dainty flowers in life's desolate sanctuary,
A spring of tranquil feelings in wisdom's sterile estuary;
The morn's sprightly smiles, the melody of moonbeams,
The song of flowing streams, as oblivated in dreams;
The secret of buds in sprout, as their motley hues spring,

The whisper of dew-drops, as on leaves they silently sing;
The portrait of sorrow, as it rolls down in idle tears,
And life's sapid spirit laced with fetter-some flowers.

Beyond the smoke, din and bustle, fatigue and dust,
Some cool and meandering stream full to the brim;
Where, beneath a bough, to rest the mind's tempest,
There to leisure away the eve and the twilight dim;
Stealing a few fleeting moments from the bustle of life,
Where Man, self-immersed, can sit *sans* moment's strife;

Baring out his heart's wishes in the peaceful bliss of solitude,
Where, in eve's shade, Man can perceive his deeds in beatitude.

Enough the mundane pleasures of the self to find,
Just a little abode do the angles desire for the mind.

Ah! Man, you are miserable; you are but destiny's face!
Ah! The son of Manu, you are your own utter disgrace!

Ye, the conqueror of Nature's mysteries beyond ken,
Frightening one and all from the welkin to the ocean;
Scaling the subtleties of Creation with intellect's depth,
Have torn asunder the atom's impregnable strength;
Why gyrating helplessly in the whirlwind of intelligence,
Whither ever do you fly, aimless and in stark ignorance?
What is the objective? What is the goal? What are the means?
Futile are science' marvels, if Man is oblivious of such themes.
You can ride the ether and eavesdrop the whispers of many a star and planet;
But can scarce call to memory's retrograde lane, a matter so small and straight.

A thing so simple and bare,
A pall of lust envelops the air.

In the forest of lechery's interminable night,

Overwhelmed by its benighted, blinding clout,
His own self man devours, ensnared by doubt;

The fragrance of sky in his mind, yet in his veins the mire of blood plies,
In speech like an angel so bright, yet in his horrible deeds an animal lies.

Man, whose planes do in the ether and beyond the horizons fly,
Shuddering in fright, at the beck of his hands, does the atom shy;
To whom, baring bosoms, the elements have revealed secrets profound,
Of peaks, oceans, the sky, or the land beneath and above the ground;
The veils are all lifted, what more chasms as yet remain unfound?
Yet Man aspires to face new impediments and to break new ground,
To ponder, act and perform, some fresh struggle on hand,
To ascend, and discover, the realm of victory's new land.

This savourless book of earth, so unendingly explored, trodden,
No more can any maiden stream bestow, its pages read so often,
A tiny book of Revelations, this great ball of earth so round,
Its copious pages galore, oft times, have men flipped around.

But Man's intellect, in such dynamic haste,
Can scarce pause to take a moment's rest;
This oft-explored land, this known book of yore,
Can it ever let new ideas blossom at Man's door?
This planet earth so tiny, its horizons so bare and narrow,
Of necessity Man requires a new world, wide and fallow.

The restless breath in Man's intellect does inwardly suffocate,
For want of ampler space, for lack of a new world to celebrate;
The planet earth, like a little ball, is too small for man's infinite goal,
Man soars upward to conquer other spheres, astride ambition's foal,
And becoming adept in science's manifold mystery,
Perchance will hold converse with Mars and Mercury.

From Man, Creation's most burnishing light,
The elements cannot hide their secrets trite;

Fierce his flame majestic, does ever so brighter reflect,
Awed and revered, alike, by the inanimate and animate;
Man, the pearl of Creation's resplendent and ever-radiant brow,
Repertoire of science, of knowledge, and of illumination's glow.

But, hearken, O Martians! If your ears can bear, then, pray, hear!
The earthly creature that perseveres to reach your distant sphere,
Is yet a savage, sanguinary and barbarian, a bare animal,
His intellect is devilish, forever aspiring the corporeal;
For when the thunderbolts of pride do quiver a man's frame so dainty,
Then, amok and afrenzy, all the rest do pour death's lethal rain aplenty.

This Man of wisdom, given to motives baser than jackals 'n' dogs,
Perpetrates acts that are heinous, and wreaks inequities and havocs,
His body, mind, and spirit, all do fight in unison,
His allies are both science and art, in annihilation;
The fruits of science, their auspicious ends in perils,
Do fester, at man's touch, and transform into devils.

Man, the reservoir of knowledge 'n' wisdom!
Man, the crown of the universal kingdom!
Heed not such epithets, weigh thy feat in contemplation;
Because man is but the minion of the lust of devastation.
Deceptive is his imagination, and his knowledge a shame,
This Man is but a colossal disgrace on humanity's name.

"All to him is known from the abyss to the sky",
But such pennants do scarce his name signify;
Laudable is the victory of his wakeful heart over mind;
Adorable is his subliminal love for the rest of his kind;
He severs the bonds of hindrance betwixt man 'n' man,
He is wise, merciful, sapient, and in sooth, a Man.

The creature whose restive mind, ever intelligent,
Tears the atom apart, but not love's impediment,

Is not Man larger than himself, small or different,
As figures in a portrait, from some unknown planet.
Perchance, from the Mars or the Saturn riven,
But aliens forever to their own spheres are driven.

Least to Man's honour, who inhabits this earth so sapful,
Are his science and his incendiary intellect so skilful;
The blazer of the world, the courier of death, the scorn of creation,
This curse of knowledge, treading upon the path of aberration.

Bewitching this strange, illusory snare of confounding prudence,
Scarce it renders Man glory for his motley, profane inventions.

Beware, Man! If science be a sword,
Then, cast it beyond memory's board.
It's proven you are a sapling innocent,
Of flowers and thorns are yet ignorant.
Sport not the sword that in your hand does dangle,
For its sharp edge will easily your limbs mangle.

This bane of science and its ills, so fierce and torrid,
Scarcely glorifies Man, who dwells this earth so sapid.
Blessed is the breeze of love that in his soul does blow,
The spirit of sacrifice that in human veins does flow.

Bliss is the stream of his rolling tears;
Bliss is his broken lute's restive cries.
The hymn of awakening, in the feelings of divine jubilation,
Glorifies Man and guides his soul to celestial peregrination.

Sacrifices, libations, abnegation of many self-gratifications,
The flame of meditation, to all these Man makes salutations.
Glorious the butter, effervescing atop the churning mind,
That softens the human heart, makes it sublime and kind.

Blessed is the benediction of science, its multitudinous discoveries,

If its winsome boons to all do reach, with accessibility and ease.
Blessed are the mind's charitable inventions for the public weal,
As they ready Nature to carry the comforts of all on her wheel,
To hold at bay the custom of human toil from wanton squander,
To yoke Nature in the service of man's happiness and grandeur.

Glorious the human skill that will equality for all create,
To fashion a new world that loving justice will consecrate;
The doubtless and unshaken belief of man in man,
To usher in the new annals of the faith-inspired man,
Shorn of the attributes of degeneration, war, and extortions,
Its pages will not be soiled nor stained by burns or distortions,
The chronicles of man will a treasure be with nectar brimful,
Whence the contentment of humanity will overflow and spill.

Exonerated from the torment and scare-fever of war,
When, in sooth, shall the earth be replete with nectar.
Blessed will be that epoch of the elegant, enlightened man,
When the land will never glimmer red with the blood of man.
Blissful will be the light of the faith unrestrained,
When man, with man, will forge a fair new bond.

The tranquil, munificent ray of equality,
When shall, O Lord! Enlighten humanity?
Imbued with soft and serene light, which forever will glisten,
When shall, O Lord! The scorched earth with new sap enliven?

CANTO - VII

Man is steeped in bonds of attachment, yet as gold is refined by fire,
Drowned deep in the dark abyss, yet does to the path of light aspire:
Striving to surge up and above, like a lotus emerging from the slush,
Or like the haloed moon, in clouds camouflaged, emerging in a hush.

Glory be to Man, though fallen deep in the abysmal pit of sin's blight,
Glory be to the virtuous son of Manu, the descendant of primeval light.
Whose faith in the brightness of hope did not succumb to the darkness,
To that great man, sacred oblations are proffered by monks countless.

The Earth lives not by the likes of men, who dread the dust,
She thrives by the deeds of those who make gold of its crust.
The ascetic escapes, being unable to bear the body's internal fire,
While life's detached connoisseur warms his cockles in this bonfire.

The way to the land of light passes through the passage of darkness,
Daybreak follows hot on the heels of netherly, nocturnal dimness,
Is there a man who has never been entrapped in sin's prison?
Whose apparel, amidst life's river, has not become sodden?

Is there a man whose path of life has perpetually been bright?
Who's so feeble as not to break free from the darkening night?
Both the sun and the moon are wary of life's orbital slips,
For both are swallowed, yet they surge beyond the eclipse.

Tumbling up and down on the path, with peaks and pits stark,

Now treading upon the earth, now riding atop virtue's steed,
The repentant sinner, battling fiercely against forces of the dark,
Makes his way majestically to the land of light, of fetters freed.

So long as tears of sorrow dwell in the eyes of man,
So long as this tale of tears grieves the heart of man,
So long as the virtues dwell in the body of everyman,
Until then humanity reposes, in sooth, its faith in Man.

Blooming on the boughs of both virtue 'n' vice, this flower of hope
Glows too in the sweltering embers of Kurukshetra's funeral pyre,
Virtuous is he who is blessed with it; he is, truly, the pious hope,
A helper of the humankind, a friend, leader, and a benevolent sire.

At last, Yudhisthira found this hope after a lot of wailing
Purging his self through repentant tears, while lamenting.
Finding the self-denying prince in the battle-field of action,
Thus spake Bhisma, brooding on Yudhisthira's perception:

"Man's ways don't culminate into Kurukshetra's funereal ashes 'n' dust,
The flower of peace, showered by tears, hereto in blossom may burst."

"Behold, O Dharmaraja! Dwapar is yielding its ground,
A Great Wave surges up to engulf an ocean unbound.
An eon is to depart from the world that lay here around,
Taking away with it the remains of all that was worth.
The good era is entombed now in its own age of birth,
Even today the flow of life proceeds on incessantly.
The past itself has collapsed in death's lap listlessly,
The future, by man's side, beckons him earnestly.

"In this battle, only the half-wrought lumps of clay
Have gone to pieces, Man's fate is not gone astray.
Man is drowned in this pool of blood, but not his humaneness,
Which sloughing off its coil lies concealed in the heart's recess.
Man's hope lies in man, O Dharmaraja! Don't seek it in vain

In the deep dark dense forest by renouncing the world of men.
Humanity puts its trust in the victor's remorseful tears,
Man's hope is nestled in the shining beads of your tears.

"Man, driven by passion, wages this battle,
Yet his thoughts remain firmly in the saddle
Of detachment; the wailing man, in utter ruins,
Is driven to his destruction by the Providence.
The passion of revenge lends a smile to man's self
The loss of humanity yet torments his inmost self.
Sweeping across the twin shores of indifference 'n' passion
The elixir of humanity is forging ahead in its own fashion.

"Diadems, realms, riches 'n' austerities, look at them without bias,
Humanity is more majestic than prayers and sacrifices of the pious.
Distinctions 'n' differences have a form, it's not for religion to find,
Any and every man is like any and every other man of his own kind.
He who has neither wealth nor strength, nevertheless is a man,
Whether wealthy or potent, he is still very much a mortal man.
Bestowed by Nature is man's life ordained,
In which there is neither disorder nor constraint.

"Not yet has man come to grasp; what a pity!
Mounting on the top of life's equity 'n' eternity,
Man's trust is not yet firm in the others of his kind,
He fears the other man in the dungeons of his mind,
Yet and forever doubting and distrusting another,
Feeding venom's malice in the mind of his brother,
In this manner, man has been advancing to this day,
Squabbling with each other all along his ticklish way.

"Countless saints and savants have tried to fathom the river of life,
Have explored for a lifetime the virtuous form of ideal human life,
The ocean had been churned up in this great endeavour only,
Many arrows of wisdom were shot to pierce the void squarely,
In search of this only men have fallen to vices,

In seeking this only have they made sacrifices,
In the quest of this a number of men became ascetic,
In pursuit of this they have waged battles annihilistic.

"Light the lamp of wisdom and seek to discover, if ye crave,
Fare forward beyond Kurukshetra's funeral fields, ye brave!
Be indifferent to worldly bonds, be a true ascetic, go and heal,
Be a beacon unto man, leading the path with sacrificial zeal,
Confer the dignity of humanity upon those in disgrace,
Make the strong shed marks of arrogance from the face,
Bestow the warmth of feeling to the frigid emotion,
And wrest the venomous potion from pride's possession.

"Pluck out the fangs so as to nip in bud the battle,
Set the earth free of the dread of wolves 'n' tigers;
Or else, let the unborn lambs be born as the tigers,
Stuff their tender teeth with venom vile 'n' fatal;
Bestow boons of blossom to many a tiny tree,
Shuddering beneath the gigantic banyan tree;
Tear off the trunk and break the boughs that cap
The titanic tree which sucks out the earth's sap.

"O Dharmaraja! This land and kingdom,
Like a bonded slave is no one's fiefdom,
All the men dwelling on this earth
Are equal to each other by birth.

"Everyone is granted the right at birth,
To sip the nourishing water of the earth,
To breathe free from want and dearth,
To live upon the earth, theirs by birth.

"One 'n' all desire the bright liberating light,
The cool breeze that soothes human plight,
All seek unfettered growth 'n' advancements
Bereft of nebulous doubts and impediments.

"All men are created much the same,
To reach the skies remains their aim,
Taste to the fullest the fruits of fame,
Be on earth to play 'n' win the game.

"But hurdles lie thick and galore,
Spread on this path many more,
Impeding the way of humanity,
Mountains stand in grim tenacity.

"As long as righteous joy is not accessible,
To each 'n' every man if it's not available,
There will not be any ease on the earth,
Until then how can peace take birth?

"As long as the share of pleasure's cake,
Among mortal men are of unequal make,
The clamour will not die down,
Nor shall the conflict calm down.

"The path was simple, marching in unity,
To savour of the pleasure in its entirety;
Not just for one's own selfish sake,
Pilfer other's piece of the pleasure-cake.

"Forgetful, man got trapped in a muddy situation,
In a mire of fright and mutual mucky suspicion,
Being absorbed in the selfsame, sensuousness
Amassing for self, pleasure 'n' lasciviousness.

"From this individualistic 'n' Epicurean gaiety
Emanated the streak of venomous felony,
Fallen in this abysmal pit, the entire humanity
Got stuck, writhing and tossing in agony.

"Joys unlimited, God-proffered,
Lie on the land wide-scattered,
Men who can relish in that mirth,
Are not enough upon this earth.

"Spread out from the land to the high skies
This life-giving water will not deplete ever;
This worthy light and fresh air do suffice,
These gifts shall not be diminished ever.

"Wealth 'n' precious stones, grains, fruits 'n' flowers,
This land bestows suchlike things from its rich stores,
Nourisher of the deer-like creatures dwelling therein,
This dense global abode is matchless in its bearing.

"These mountains with lofty and stainless peaks
Have diamond-like jewels filled in its creeks,
These oceans that nourish on its rich floor,
Many a purest gem, pearls 'n' corals galore.

"And the ever new curiosity of man
Do new hopes and dreams inspire,
His potent arms, wide in their span,
Adept in churning oceanic reservoir.

"The ever-exploring, wandering human mind
That gropes forward even in the pitch dark,
To find Nature's novel forms of many kind,
That each day opens shrouded secrets stark.

"Against these mighty arms 'n' wisdom
Is there anything that can withstand?
Can any glory elude man's kingdom?
Can it remain away from his hand?

"So many radiant and latent treasures
Lie in the lap of the Mother Nature,

All could relish the coveted pleasures
Relishing heartily the earth's flavour.

"All could taste of satiation equal,
All could enjoy pleasures equal,
If only they wished; then, in a twinkle,
Could make earth a heaven, it's simple.

"All the realities of essence, in sooth,
God keeps concealed from untruth,
By arduous endeavour 'n' tardy struggle,
Man has found them without any trouble.

"Mankind's destiny or his fate
Is not writ by Brahma's[1] *diktat*
He has reached the ecstatic state of beatitude
With his mighty arms 'n' unyielding attitude.

"Never does Nature stoop in mortal fear
To the forces of fate, hearken ye dear!
All the time it yields, however,
To man's enterprise 'n' labour.

"The secret inscriptions of Brahma, the divine creator
Tend to be deciphered only by the slothful creature,
The valiant neaten the mark off their broad forehead
By the beads of sweat over their eyebrows spread.

"Fatalism is but the sheath of sin 'n' transgression
A weapon used for mankind's utter exploitation,
Through which a man enthralls by suppression,
The portion of another man in the civilization.

"Ask any of the fatalists as such
If the force of fate is that much?
Why the gems that lie in the earth's inmost root
Do not spring of their own onto a man's foot?

"Why did man make riches out of mean matter,
By nourishing Nature with his sweat, and water?
Couldn't man, just like that, lift these up straight,
The treasures amassed by the force of his fate?

"And when he ceased to be, in the yester birth,
After hoarding a fortune on the planet earth,
When he left behind his sons and spouse,
Did he entrust it to anyone else's house?

"The place where he took birth one day,
The realm over which he rules today,
Is it the same home? And, tell me first,
Is this treasure part of the same trust?

"Ask him, too, when he had, O ye dear!
Gathered the riches, that very first year,
Behind that hoard of abundant wealth,
What fateful sequence worked in stealth?

"The same milking of man's labours rigourous,
The selfsame exploitation, downright iniquitous,
The very same guile to fox the human society,
The selfsame acquisition, the sordid dis-piety.

"One man pieces together his riches,
Driven by the force of sinful wishes,
While the other relishes it with mirth,
In the guise of fatalism on the earth.

"One and same is the destiny of human society,
That is his labour; and his arms that are mighty,
Before which lies prostrate the earth in humility
To which the skies too offer their salute in reality.

"One who has pledged his sweat 'n' labour
Don't let him lag behind and not savour,

Let him be the first and the foremost,
Deriving from nature pleasures utmost.

"Whatever riches are imbued in Nature,
Lie at man's sweet disposing pleasure
O Dharmaraja! Each bit of every atom,
Belongs to every man in the macrocosm.

"Safe would it have been, to have better stayed,
All the mundane rights of the common head,
The state of the world would have surely been
Unlike the grim panorama being presently seen.

"Labour would have been the dearest treasure,
All would have earned a lot of this pleasure,
All would have been drunk of this leisure,
All would have luxuriated in heady measure.

"No king or commoner would be there
Being a man would have mattered here,
Had man not writ fate upon his palm,
Arduous would have stayed his arm.

"Who is sovereign over anyone up here?
Who is subject to someone? O ye dear!
Man misled by the selfsame, utter illusion,
Has begotten for his self much confusion.

"Just as water and fire are easily attainable
Without curb or encumbrance to all;
Land, too, was likewise readily available
Once, without strife, to one and all.

"Man was the lover of man, his brother
Each one had abiding faith in the other
Non-possession, thy name was the law,
People were wedded to action, *sans* flaw.

"Bonded in the thread of religion
All men lived in joyful unison,
Sharing the grief of their brethren,
Amidst ever cheerful expression.

"No distinction of rank was at all there;
Equity reigned among men everywhere;
Humankind was knit together in relation,
All men loved one another *sans* aberration.

"One and all toiled upto the hilt of their intent,
Consumed the needful to their heart's content,
Never did anyone esteem his self above the rest,
As though he was special or better than the best.

"Pledged were they all to civil ligaments,
No one dwelt in idiosyncratic fragments,
No man's pleasure was in anyway different,
From the current of society's predicament.

"No one was worried about amassing pelf
For the greater good of one's own self;
Or pilfer the morsel from humanity,
And stuff his abode with vain vanity.

"There was neither any ruler, nor any ruled,
Nor was there any regime, strictly principled,
Morality was the primal fashion of mankind,
Sheer discipline reigned over every human mind.

"The rights of man are now secured by law
By virtue of the judicial code and its awe;
All humane things then one could in full measure find,
In the self-righteous conduct of the early humankind.

"The path of life was quite simple,

On all sides freedom was ample,
No step was bound by impediments
Of customs and regal statements.

"Targets desirable, according to his wish,
A man could naturally well accomplish.
The glorious summit of self perfection,
He could reach without any trepidation.

"And then came the evil spirit of Kali age,
That entered as lust into man's mental cage;
And then the vile venom of greed spread
Stealthily into man's life, begetting dread.

"Then, hard times struck and people perished
The minds of survivors were distraught;
Then, from a corner of the heart, as yet hid,
Spake the greed of man with lust fraught.

"Alas! Had ye kept your humane resource
In safe custody, and followed the right course;
Then, in this crucial hour would ye easy lie,
Then, ye would not at all have to rue and cry.

"Calamity would not have befallen all,
Nor would it have taken ye as its toll,
Awake, ye fool, for hard times to come,
Feather your nest before chaos is come.

"And man gradually awakened, goaded by remorse,
But falsely awoke, embarked on a selfish course,
Ventured to pile up untold riches 'n' wealth,
Hidden from the others, gathered in stealth.

"To whichever direction one man set out,
All men 'n' women followed him without doubt;

Then, each began to safeguard himself in isolation,
Each braced up silently, in meaningful preparation.

"The serpent of greed hissed evil venom off its fangs,
Thenceforth poured out theft 'n' such other wrongs,
Plunder, scuffles, abuse 'n' assault made headway,
Insolence, snatch 'n' grab, coercion held the sway.

"The immanent benign order was shattered to pieces
The existing social paradigm was plagued with vices,
Thence started the turmoil, creating a wide furore,
The poor earth began to tremble, all was topsy-turvy.

"And then came the sword into the fray
To douse the earth that in flames lay,
To contain the all-consuming greed
Of mankind and their entire breed.

"And the valiant sword-wielding man
Became the master of common man,
A despot, vested with legal authority,
In truth, a demon disguised in human body.

"Man set out, forsaking the society,
To satiate the self in a state of gaiety,
Tumbled headlong, though at random,
Into the abysmal depth of thralldom.

"The natural love of one man for another
Won't have died on the earth, O brother!
Had man, ceding dishonesty, been repentant
To his kinsfolk and to many a dependent.

"If man had been true to the golden treasure
Of firm, unshaken faith in other brothers;
Had he not been forgetful of the others
By immersing himself in selfish pleasure.

"Had he been careful of his clan,
That he is naught else, but a Man;
A wise son of Manu, truly the very best,
Of a species above beasts 'n' birds of nest.

"Then, never would he have found solace
In losing the glory of being of human race,
In bowing timidly before any regal seal,
In being a slave under the royal heel.

"He who could not bear the soft,
Natural bonds of love, times oft,
Lies the same man, now enchained,
In the tentacles of the law of the land.

"A man who could not bestow upon another
Out of love and care, a part of his pleasure,
Has to cede the same, now under the fear
Of the grim and awesome royal sceptre.

"Ignoring the call of justice and truth,
Treating both with disdain, in sooth,
Comprehends now in fear each 'n' every word
Spoken in the language of the dazzling sword.

"Can the decadence of the human race
Go further down the abyss in disgrace?
Could the sanctity of human dignity
Be defiled to yet greater profanity?

"The tribe of mankind is in utter need
Of a sword-wielding despot, indeed,
A kind tyrant set out to do his very best
Whom wayward men fear in real earnest.

"A despot is direly needed, for
Men fight others with sharp claws,

A sabre is justly sought, for
Men scarcely fear the coded laws.

"A king is rightly called for, at least
To herd men together, as many a beast,
To restrain them from acts nasty,
To train them in ethics 'n' modesty.

"A king is really needed by mankind,
To skew humanity's foolhardy mind,
To sprinkle water every moment,
To douse flames of mutual dissent.

"Indeed, humanity deserves a Chief,
Or else, they would do battle to the hilt,
And die, fighting to finish, in grief,
Engulfed in one-another's blood of guilt.

"Monarchy is indicative of man's stature,
Of his deficient 'n' mean human nature,
Of a pathetic and unrepentant humanity,
Of the vileness of human culture 'n' dignity.

"Monarchy came into being to act as a bulwark,
To halt the stride of the ever-advancing vice,
It came not to draw up a defining peripheral mark,
Or, to confine the free man's virtues nice.

"Lo and behold! The new daily chores,
Ideas have now a prescribed course,
Not to mention actions discordant with law,
Even thinking of such thoughts is held in awe?

"Be it Krishna or Vidur(2), whosoever he may be,
All are bound to canons of disciplined behavior,
Upon their thought, speech and action, all three,
Lies a chain of consistent, formal, social order.

"If their actions too deviate to a different course,
That which is not in tune with the authority,
They too would be of trifling value, of course,
Just like a straw before the royal authority.

"Safeguarding the natural order of things
Is the cardinal end that all authority seeks.
It cannot let that natural order go astray
From the path of life's idealistic sway.

"So, voices contrary to convention none could raise,
None could dare to utter any blame or any praise,
Even the instance of sacred codes of compassion
None could give vent to his wishful expression.

"Bearing upon his neck the terrible stone
Of an imperious system acting on its own;
Man is roaming about in the universe,
Forgetting his real self and purpose.

"Man could not keep control over his mind
And live in peace with the rest of his kind;
Hence, he made the sabreur his keeper,
To safeguard his own living sphere.

"And today this stern sentinel
Does not allow men to yell,
Nor stray away from tradition,
Nor let him blossom to fruition.

"Man, however, by his many an evil deed,
Made it possible for the king to succeed;
By picking up wanton quarrels mutually,
Allowed the king to be anointed duly.

"So long as the rock-hard greedy selfishness,
Remains enkindled in the heart's crevices,

Till then, the king, sabreur, and the sentinel,
Cannot be dispensed with by men, in general.

"Men became unruly, and hence needed a ruler
Who could hold aloft the banner of righteousness;
Monarchy is a created evil. indeed it is peculiar,
Hence, regal laws seem to be heavy duteousness.

"O Dharmaraja! Seeking a life, ascetic 'n' chaste,
Is cowardice of the mind, a great frailty;
The essence of humanity, its real earnest test,
Lies in solving life's problems in reality.

"It's not indeed beyond man's reach
To satisfy the self, individually;
It's arduous however to gratify each,
And the countless, collectively.

"There is a Path that says: *forsake the world*,
And immerse the self into the selfsame,
Seeking freedom only for self in this world,
And let joy of the self be thy only aim.

"There is another Path: *ignite the others*
By the spark of reason ingrained in you,
Reach the heavens with your brothers,
Taking many of them along with you.

"The devout austerity with which ye intend
To obtain pleasures only for your self-gain;
The same austerity that makes man a saint,
Can remove the sorrows of countless men.

"Keeping your perfections treasured in the self,
Doesn't behove the aim of justice quite in itself;
Is it the right way for your social betterment,
To hold your attainments in self-concealment?

"O Yudhisthira! Don't in thy own self immerse,
Throw an encompassing glance at the universe,
At men engrossed in peace 'n' pleasant things,
And at everyman eager for these very things.

"Agreed that the peace ye seek in your mind
In the serene forest shall ye absolutely find,
But what footprints would ye leave behind
Here on this earth, for the rest of mankind?

"Perchance, relief from grief you may get
In the dense recesses of the deep forest,
But where shall mankind take refuge,
From this combustible world so huge?

"And if the self-abnegating ideal set by you
Is imbibed by the people, in its truest hue;
Humankind could settle then in woods anew,
Being uprooted from their worldly milieu.

"The populous land would become a cremation ground
And the palace would dissolve in desolation unbound;
The fretful world by which the hermit is hounded,
To the same world in the woods he shall be grounded.

"Perchance, even there too, if the townsfolk
Settle, upset by worldly troubles that choke,
Then the hermit shall have to escape the deeps
Of the forest, taking the holy pot that he keeps.

"O Dharmaraja! Does the hermit ever flee,
Away from his home or dense forest?
In fact, he escapes from the melee,
Indeed, from life's unyielding unrest.

"He longs ever for pleasures pleasant,
Shunning all things that are pungent,

Always and ever desirous for gain,
Eever ever wants to loose in vain.

"He dwells in revelry, winning trophies for his side,
But wears a gloomy face, when he kisses the dust,
He smiles invariably in growth, ever with leery lust,
But wails bitterly when decay comes in his stride.

"He just cannot stay calm and neutral,
Frets, wails, and gets restless in real,
Thinks as to why the life that he leads
Doesn't conform to the wishes he pleads.

"But life, however, is inlaid intricately
Into a framework exceedingly comely,
In how many moulds could it be cast?
For itself to re-create in patterns vast.

"One who clears the shrubs and fells the forest,
Can diligently pave of his own a path surest;
Life is not a slave to somebody,
It cannot be owned by anybody.

"O Yudhisthira! Life is not for them who are in throes,
Who encounter its challenges with fear and dismay,
Life belongs indeed to those valiant and brave heroes
Who battle fearlessly, fighting with firm feet in the fray.

"This ocean changes everyone's cozy countenance
Displeases all with the taste of its bitter brine,
But it offers nectar to those who, with perseverance,
Churn the ocean of life with a vigour fine.

"He who wishes to have the nectar for free,
Without ascending the tip of the high tree;
He longs in vain to relish the nectar divine,
Who can't bear the brunt and stays supine.

"Denouncing the ocean of life as salty
He goes away from life's proximity.
Nectar, wine, and many a precious stone,
Such treasures he turns his back upon.

"He flees away from the toil of life's dance,
Seeing in his mind's eye, that perchance,
He would get the treasure of pleasures grand
Lying scattered somewhere in the woodland.

"He wishes to acquire the treasure-trove at one go,
Longs for all things coming in his thoughts' flow;
He thinks, as from his home does he advance,
Things will roll down to his feet, as if by chance.

"O Dharmaraja! It is, forsooth, an utter defeat,
In man's battle with life, a cowardly retreat;
To flee to forest where peace reigns unbound,
Hounded by the crowded world lying around.

"Such renunciation in fact smacks of remorse,
It gives stimulus to escape, and so is despicable,
It's not worth toiling for, nor is the proper course,
It's an illusion of the vanquished mind, unstable.

"It finds escape from the clamour,
By turning a deaf ear to its murmur;
It finds the path that saves from fire
By turning its back, intent to retire.

"Fearful even of the air spread around,
It hides the feeble austerity profound,
Delving deep into the dim darkness,
Forsakes life's tempestuous distress.

"Fleeing from the world of action,
It settles in one's own bower,

And eyes in fanciful imagination,
Dreams of heaven's flower.

"That dream which bears no mark
Of the finger-print of reality quite,
That dream which has no spark
Of a blazing life, shining bright.

"That land of dreams, lovely 'n' dainty,
Where only flowers blossom aplenty,
Where the dance of the dust has no sway,
Nor a thorn ever encountered on the way.

"Not things bitter, we all are aware,
Only the sweet 'n' soft exist there,
Where iron melts and becomes mellow,
Becomes the light of moon with a halo.

"Where the *diktats* of rosy imagination,
Swell the waves in the life's ocean,
Events unfold there in the same fashion,
As are dear to vision's fanciful motion.

"Ask the man, who is truly indifferent,
That what he sees in the mind's eye?
Isn't the world he conceives a figment?
Where on this earth does it really lie?

"Where indeed is the blessed alley
That abounds with flowers only?
Where indeed is that favoured pathway,
Where feet do not come in harm's way.

"Where dwells that ever-blooming green?
That wondrous verdant garden serene?
Where in the skies lies the speck-less region?
Which is not swamped by the dust of action.

"He seceded into the cocoon of his bleary thought,
Turning away from the battles he should've fought;
Could the world become free of grief,
By clinging to his self-thought relief.

"And let him admit *sans* compunction,
Is he not verily duty-bound to action?
For, even to live, by alms a-begging,
He's indeed to do some labouring.

"The whole world is a theatre of action
So long as on the earth lives a person,
Till then the sense of duty does thrive,
Lies ensconced in each atom of life.

"By forsaking the core law of action,
How could a man find satisfaction?
The law of action shall forever stay,
No matter wherever he gets away.

"O Dharmaraja! The path of assiduous man
Does not lie in renunciation, in being wan;
That upon which treads man, a mortal,
Is the concrete earth, not a skied portal.

"The thoughts that ye harbour today
In your mind's recesses with dismay,
The course of action that ye now devise,
Shall take ye away from life, it's unwise.

"Great indeed is the emancipation of the self;
But it is still far better for the lamp to help
Spread indeed the light for all, far and wide,
Flames that dispel darkness in their stride.

"Your detachment keeps you in illusion,
Is infirm 'n' decrepit, in morbid confusion,

Forsooth, it is the reflection of lassitude,
A stratagem played by wisdom's platitude.

"O Yudhisthira! Shield thyself from negative impression,
It may sink you into the dark abyss of mental cogitation,
The venomous fume of placid inaction,
Could imbue your life with fatal potion.

"The detachment that disgust breeds,
Is a sudden upsurge of a weak mind,
He that flees on the thought's steeds,
Would not return, nor his home find.

"It reiterates life as fleeting,
Deems slumber as awakening,
And thus makes life insipid,
Seeing life as death is frigid.

"It values non-existence as an entity,
Decrees losses to be gains aplenty,
It holds those actions as the best,
Which prompt a man into inert rest.

"It proclaims only that to be truly real
Which, alien to senses, is unattainable,
It sees the perceptible as illusory fraction,
Although therein lies the natural action.

"It abets indolence to thrive in all
By the succour of lamentation,
It causes the tree of life to fall,
In the guise of renunciation.

"It can't bear the sound, sweet 'n' soft
That stems from the world of action,
It quells thus by various ways, oft,
The fire blazing in man's passion.

"A renunciate's detached smile stealthily it steals
The fragrance of flowers that a soft kiss feels;
And arrests the forward quiver of dew drops
By the thought that from renunciation crops.

"Melodic lyrics stay not so strong,
In the heart of the soaring bird,
The flute plays not the song,
In tune with emotions stirred.

"It says in whispers even to many a tender leaf,
'Ye need not grow, for growth is veritable grief;'
It says, destroying the self is the greatest liberation,
In withering away lies truly the real gratification.

"Scaring the flowers, blooming in their pink,
By disclosing the surety of life's mortal link;
It disillusions Beauty's aesthetic rhyme,
Considering it as fodder 'n' feed of Time.

"Prosperity, beauty, splendour and pleasures,
Detachment divests man of all these treasures;
It emaciates and enfeebles every person,
Reducing him to an object of compassion.

"Not only it drains the zeal away
From the life-breath of heroes,
It saps their strength, in a way,
The fatal flash of radiant arrows.

"O Dharmaraja! All know the crux,
That creation is in a state of flux,
Is there, in sooth, any man on earth,
Who could defy death after his birth?

"But if the state of transience does roam,
Pervading man, as a psychic syndrome,

His eyes can never see any variety,
Other than clear, crude ephemerality.

"The man who stays in utter foolhardy dejection
How can he do his job with selfless devotion?
Equipping the self, although with ambivalent mind,
How can he wage the war, in confusion entwined?

"He who disregards the turmoil
Of life, and the consequent toil,
Who in a calm meditative pose,
Is obsessed with death's throes.

"That passive man full of gloom,
Could he ever proffer any help?
Here, down on this earthen shelf,
Could he help a flower to bloom?

"Ever shall that brooding man this fancy keep,
That the face of the earth is but mortal,
That to labour is an error, it is better to sleep,
Does a flower ever live a life eternal?

"Forsaking the world, he roams around,
Seeking for his own self immortal glory,
But is swallowed by the maws unbound
And mortality then ends his life's story.

"The way of the world goes on,
Keeps moving ever forward on;
Life's flame keeps glowing ever,
Relieving the burdens of the other.

"The tattered petals of faded flowers wither,
And fresh buds blossom hither and thither,
Some pilgrims in the caravan drop midway
And new ones join the lot on the pathway.

"An indolent scholar does not become immortal,
By reproaching his heart in lamentation,
The age of a mortal diminishes not from the total,
By bearing the labour of duty's action.

"O Yudhisthira! This much distinction does exist
Between the twain kinds of mankind at least,
The man of action laughs off his toil in zest,
The other one laments, seeks refuge in forest.

"There is a kind of man that adorns the earth,
With blossomed lotuses, blooming in mirth,
Affluence 'n' charms he brings to the world,
By the power of his own potency unfurled.

"Braving the muck and slime of the earth,
Enduring the various afflictions of birth,
Dallying with the dazzling sublime light,
Floating aloft the dark waves of the night.

"Wading the inaccessible earth 'n' fathomless sea,
He unleashes blissfully the life-giving sap of earth,
He beats the kettle-drum in his delirious ecstasy
Singing paeans to humanity's triumphant worth.

"He bids adieu to the world at last,
Making it a better place in every sense,
Leading the world beyond the past,
Beyond the juncture he started whence.

"The other one shuts himself up in the mansion
Of thoughts profound, but bereft of action,
Searching, vainly, for the shores in the ocean,
Sans ship or sails, bracing the waves' motion.

"Somehow he nourishes the God-given body,
Living off alms got from men bound in duty,
Declaring himself to be ever detached and holy,
Declares the entire world as mundane 'n' lowly.

"He goes round uttering, as if on a sermonizing spree:
The guile of illusion is spread so far as eyes could see;
Whatever is invisible, imperceptible and unattainable,
Only the Truth abides; verily, the Reality is ineffable.

"As if this body, this field of action,
Indeed is an illusory bit, a fraction,
As if all the virtues of man 'n' his glory
Are but delusions incarnate and hoary.

"As if by giving up action and deed,
Man could, of his own lot, be freed.
Deserting the populated land in haste,
As if he could make the sky his nest.

"As if sin underlies the very act of birth,
As if men fall from heaven on the earth;
As if to lessen the load of man's past action,
Thence to pave the way for further fruition.

"Sight, taste, hearing, touch and odour:
Sins lurk in these five senses, as it were,
As if the tongue, skin, eye, ear and nose,
Are not allies, but the most wicked foes.

"The path of salvation unfolds itself,
Forsooth, as if by killing the self,
As though life's terrestrial course,
Cannot be reached by material force.

"As if this whole created world,
Is but some sudden occurrence,

As if no purpose is involved,
In man's coming into existence.

"O Dharmaraja! The world is surely transient,
What blame do I incur, if it is evanescent?
All have been made to descend here;
None has come on his own over here.

"Had the fate of man not been so utterly miserable
That he had to be moulded from the earth perishable,
Born would he have been in species ethereal,
Perchance, in the skies, in forms incorporeal.

"He would have become surely one with the rays,
Bereft of attachment, of hungry and thirsty ways;
Staying free of action's bondage, free in spirit,
Devoid of ears, eyes, arms and the moving feet.

"But life on the earth is beset with adversity,
Man succumbs to hungers 'n' cravings petty,
The sensation and pulsations of the mind,
Do arouse abject thirsts of many a kind.

"The fire of the belly, this unquenchable thirst,
Does not let a man relax, by hunger cursed,
It ever coaxes the mind to thoughtful worry,
Sends his arms towards action in a hurry.

"A heaven in the mind is in vain,
It's an Eden the body can't obtain,
That paradise is definitely great,
Which man's arms do itself create.

"For whatever the arms bring along,
The mind too savours it before long,
Bare meditation, unknown to the arms,
Even to the mind, it remains in qualms.

"Effective are the arms that overwhelm the mind too,
With ripples of joy surging in incessant succession.
Successful is that meditation, a silhouette of the True,
Of which even the arms could happily take possession.

"There, where lies the path of pure action,
And another of contemplation 'n' reflection,
Contours of that life, eclipsed by dualistic semblance,
Do not unfold its true meaning in full efflorescence.

"By flying upon the wings of hoary wisdom,
Man could scarce surmount life's dilemma,
The thirst of mind is diminished very seldom
By retiring from the world's varied panorama.

"There is no external foe, waiting in right earnest,
In fear of whom man could escape to the forest,
Wherever to ye may proceed, there shall ye find,
That this foe dwells in the recesses of the mind.

"But the foes that the hermit conquers,
By renouncing the worldly rancours,
O Dharmaraja! You may win them, too,
By adopting the ways of the world in true.

"That which a wilful, stubborn ascetic slays,
By subduing the self in many gradual ways,
You too could tame that alive, by your restraint,
By making the self obey your commandment.

"And that which could never be obtained,
By an ascetic wedded to detachment,
You could attain that blissful enchantment,
While staying in the world in restraint.

"The pleasure that accrues to the man,
Who mingles freely with one and all,

By rejoicing in the joy of everyman,
And standing by them when they fall.

"The merit which accrues by extending help
To those who are limbless and without pelf;
The merit derived from bearing the burden
Of people who are quite helpless and fallen.

"Not that woods only have pretty and fair lands,
Behold this bounteous earth, as if in a trance!
Seeking relief, at each and every step, stands
Penury, in doleful dejection, awaiting a chance.

"The earth needs corn, raiment 'n' water,
And aspires earnestly for hopes pious;
The earth requires feet 'n' arms vigorous,
And craves for the speaking power.

"It seeks the bewitching glimpse of that sight
That you have already, forsooth, perceived,
It seeks the goal you have already achieved,
Reaching whereupon, you rest after the fight.

"O Dharmaraja! By the dread of that fear,
Which laid you to renounce life's sphere;
Ye see now in that raging inferno universal,
The harrowing sight of the world terrestrial.

"If renunciation is a sure anodyne
Why conceal this ambrosial wine?
To the distraught, teach the notion,
Of your magical axiom of salvation.

"Go and pacify! By thy self-mortification,
The blazing fire of man's flaring passion,
Sprinkle the rejuvenating 'n' life-giving nectar
Upon the scorched earth, to satiate the mother.

"Don't bestow the rights of the throne,
O Yudhisthira! To woods in wilderness,
Perceive actions that are your own,
Tighten up your mind that lies in distress.

"Afflicted by arrows, the country trembles,
And the land of Bharat lies a shambles,
'Save me! Deliver me!' Resonated calls,
Emanate from breaths of countless souls.

"Tumult prevails, terror sinks the breath,
And catastrophe rules the roost today,
Emerging from the calamity of death,
The people all round suffer in dismay.

"By forsaking them and taking refuge in the forest
What peace, befitting your nature, would you wrest?
By abandoning here the service of the animate,
Can you take up the cause of the inanimate?

"Wipe off your tears, proceed in right earnest,
Go toward the world, not toward the forest,
Strive to become the guiding beacon of light,
For all men who dare for the righteous fight.

"Selfless action beckons you,
One that holy *Gita* preaches you,
With afflicted eyes moist with dew,
The strife-torn earth cries for you.

"This aggrieved and forlorn world has to be
Made to drink the nectar of the benign bee,
In the countless clusters of many a plant and sapling,
Flowers of all hues need to bloom and keep blooming.

"Your kinsfolk and many a man of mortal herd,
Whose tears have to be nipped before they burst;

Their cheery smiles need to be truly restored,
To the countless quivering lips of the horde,

"Life does not have any hold upon
Those, O Dharmaraja! Who are gone;
The alive and the kicking have to bear
The burden of this very earthy sphere.

"After Suyodhana's death, you have got
This liability coming to your destined lot,
Who else can manage it, except for you,
Who else can take its care, save for you.

"Dedicate yourself to your duties on this ground,
Evolve yourself into an ascetic, to action bound;
Man would attain naught, and become naught,
If he were forever to dwell in ethereal thought.

"Non-existence, a void absolute, reigns supreme above,
Nothingness is spread all round in the skies high above,
O Dharmaraja! Whatever exists in the universe,
Lies ensconced in the soil, in life's each verse.

"By attaining it fully and in a meticulous way,
Man garners everything under his sole sway,
To the conqueror of the earth's glorious crown,
The firmaments too, of their own, stoop down.

"Relish the resources of earth in such a manner,
That stains don't besmirch its cover 'n' banner;
Don't blend yourself into the earth's hue,
And let the selfsame be soaked in you.

"And preach this noble gospel to each 'n' everybody,
To one and all, leaving nobody in any way behind,
That they ought to steep their bodies in the *mind*,
And not allow their minds to merge into the *body*.

"The day supremacy of mind comes to prevail
Over the body of man, and follows its trail;
The day the ideal of sacrifice holds its reign
Over life, treading upon the joyous terrain.

"The day man deems gold not as an end in itself,
Perceives it just as a means to nurture his self;
The day man recognizes in its true entireness
That beauteous form of the human wholeness;

"Craving neither the crown, nor the hermitage,
Staying poised betwixt the two, in camouflage;
The true spirit, dwelling in deep recess,
That stays above the ways of the flesh.

"The day when fairly enlightened becomes mankind,
To envisage things by the very spark of wisdom,
The day when his vision would not be entwined,
Either in the hermit's robes or in the king's diadem.

"That day the morn would arise, with a crimson cap,
Heralding the ascent of man's good deserved hap;
That great dawn the conch-shells would blow free,
Telling many tell-tale tales of man's Pyrrhic victory.

"O Dharmaraja! The land of destination is yet far away,
Fritter no time, do not procrastinate, nor brook delay,
A sea of humanity has been treading ever on the way
Steer it forward and farthermost, lest it go astray.

"Man is oft and betimes a great sinner, in sooth,
That man does slaughter man is a universal truth.
But, forget not, that man for man's utter help,
Also, and ever, has been sacrificing himself.

"Greed, malice, vengeance, and animosity,
Such obstacles to manhood are in sight,

Sacrifice, abnegation, and devout austerity
The props of such things, too, are infinite.

"Inspire every other living creature,
By the vigour of your own character,
Instill a ray of virtue into the people,
By austerities that ye have ample.

"Do not keep brooding all the time,
Of man being engrossed in crime,
Alas! After the commission of a sin,
Man weeps in repentance of that sin.

"These bewailings, these tears foretell,
That the noble hope of man is yet well,
It points surely towards the cardinal fact,
That humanity is not dead, it is yet intact.

"It is not good for man's fame,
To flare in sin's blazing flame,
The right way is to gather its force
And march ahead without remorse.

"The very prop of the world does not rest solely
On the shining haloes of the doer of deeds holy;
The ray that is entrapped in the pervading darkness,
Is the earth's very hope, would free her from harness.

"Pearls of tears dwell on many a flower,
Hopes dwell in those tears that shower,
That this life is evanescent and earthy,
That such-like approach to life is pithy.

"O Dharmaraja! If ye keep the torch of hope ahead,
The earth will sure become free of war's dread.

Men won't plunge for long into the pool of passion,
Life won't forever be served by immoral injunction.

Human haloes can barely be eclipsed by defeat on the land,
And man's grace is scarce enhanced by trophies in hand.

Sacrifice of love 'n' affection would be a sin for humanity,
Heaven shall the earth become with the dawn of civility."

NOTES

CANTO-I

1. Kuru: A mythological king of the lunar dynasty of Kshatriyas (warriors), after whom the clan of Kauravas was named.
2. Bhima: One of the five Pandava brothers who had fulfilled his vow by drawing blood from the breast of a Kaurava Prince (Duhsshasna).
3. Draupadi: Daughter of king Drupad wedded to Pandavas, the sons of Pandu, an ancient king of Hastinapur.
4. Drona: The preceptor of the Kuru princes, both Kauravas and Pandavas; his son, Ashwathama, supposedly immortal, wore a jewel on his forehead.
5. Kauravas: The descendants of the king Kuru, representing the vanquished party amongst the belligerents in the Great Indian War (Mahabharata).
6 Dhritrashtra: The blind Kuru king of Hastinapur (modern Delhi).
7. Pandavas: The five valiant sons of king Pandu, and the heroes of *Mahabharata* (Yudhisthira, Bhima, Arjuna, Nakul, and Sahdeva).
8. Suyodhana: The elder son of Dhritrashtra, the Kuru king; better known as Duryodhana.
9. Yudhisthira: The eldest son of Pandu (Dhritrashtra's deceased brother, and former king of Hastinapur); also the legitimate heir to the Kuru throne.
10. Abhimanyu: A martyred son of Arjuna, the third of the Pandava brothers, who was killed by stratagem in the Mahabharata war.
11. Parth: One of the ten names of Arjuna, the great archer and disciple of Lord Krishna.
12. Pitamaha: Literally, grandfather/great-grandfather; used for Bhisma, the regent of the Kauravas.

CANTO-II

1. Vyas: Veda Vyas, the writer of *Mahabharata*, a celebrated ancient Indian sage and savant.
2. Dharmaraja: One of the names of Yudhisthira, the eldest of the Pandavas, and famous for righteousness.
3. Uttara: Spouse of Abhimanyu, the martyred young son of Arjuna.
4. Krishna: A kin of the Kurus and a maternal cousin of Pandavas; regarded as the eighth of the ten incarnations of Vishnu (a Hindu god), who supported the Pandavas in the war without wielding arms, being Arjuna's charioteer.
5. *Gita*: "The Song Celestial": it forms the core of the Mahabharata epic; most commonly known as the *Bhagvad-Gita* containing the celebrated discourse of Lord Krishna directed to Arjuna, the brave but doubting hero of *Mahabharata*; also see 'Foreword'.
6. Kurukshetra: See 'Foreword'.
7. Kaunteya: Refers here to Yudhisthira, the son of Kunti. Bhima and Arjuna also referred to as Kaunteya, being the two other sons of Kunti.
8. Bhisma: Great-grand uncle of the Kaurava and Pandava princes and the Regent of the Hastinapur kingdom.
9. Rama: Ramchandra, the exiled prince of Ayodhya and the hero of the *Ramayana*, the greatest Sanskrit epic alongside *Mahabharata;* the greatest of the Indian kings of the solar dynasty; also regarded as the seventh incarnation of Vishnu (a Hindu god).
10. Sita: The celebrated daughter of King Janak (of Mithila) who was married to Rama, the hero of the renowned Indian epic *Ramayana*.

CANTO-III

1. Bharat: A mythological Aryan king who ruled the lands that later came to be known as Bharatvarsha, after whom the name Bharat (India) came in vogue.
2. The story in Mahabharata relates that the Kauravas conspired to minister poison to Bhima, the bravest of the Pandava brothers, but somehow he was saved.
3. Shellac-house; Kauravas, aided by Shakuni (Duryodhana's maternal uncle), plotted to kill the Pandava brothers by making arrangements for their stay, during a forest retreat, in a house built of shellacs, an inflammable material. The shellac-house was burnt in the night at the behest of Kauravas, but the Pandavas had escaped.

4. Raghupati: one of the many names of Lord Rama, the incarnation of Lord Vishnu in Hindu mythology.
5. Jarasandha: The demon king of Magadha (modern Bihar) and a sworn enemy of Lord Krishna and the Pandavas.

CANTO-IV

1. Radheya: A name of Karna, the loyal friend of Duryodhana and a might warrior; sworn enemy of the Pandavas.
2. Drupada: Father of Draupadi, the spouse of Pandavas.
3. Shakuni: Prince of Gandhara and the maternal uncle of Duryodhana, who plotted to bring about the destruction of Pandavas.
4. Shishupal: A wicked king slaughtered by Lord Krishna.
5. Rajasuya Sacrifice: A consecration ritual performed by the great kings in ancient India to establish their supremacy over other kings in the *Aryavarta*, the land of the Aryans. It was a typical sacrifice in olden times which, when successfully performed by a king, entitled him to the designation of an Emperor.
6. Keshava: One of the many names of Lord Krishna.
7. Indraprastha: The name of Pandava kingdom in modern Meerut (near Delhi). Due to the internecine feud between the Kauravas and the Pandavas for the Kuru throne, the Hastinapur kingdom (modern Delhi) was divided into Hastinapur and Indraprastha. The latter was developed as a capital by the Pandavas when they were driven out of Hastinapur.
8. Dharma: Righteousness; Natural Order; Social Law.
9. Karma: Providence; Destiny; Law of Cause and Effect.

CANTO-V

1. Sharade: An invocation to the goddess of learning in Indian mythology.
2. Dwapar: Name of the third of the four Yugas (Eons) of Creation, according to Hindu mythology. The other three are Satyuga, Krityuga (Tretayuga) and Kaliyuga.
3. Kali: Refers to Kaliyuga, the fourth eon of time, according to Hindu mythology, reigning during the present time.
4. *Vedas*: The earliest extant records of human knowledge in the Indic tradition. There are four Vedas: Rig, Sam, Yajur, and Atharva.
5. Manu: The first created Man, like the Adam of western mythology.

CANTO-VI

1. Varunesh: The Lord of the Oceans.

CANTO-VII

1. Brahma: The Lord who created the universe.
2. Vidur: Uncle of Pandavas and Kauravas in the epic *Mahabharata*, known for his wisdom.